Road to El Roi

A Journey to
The God Who Sees

Jess Moravian
Special Contribution by
Rabbi Jonathan Kligler

Edited by K. L. Walters

Copyright © Jess Moravian

All rights reserved. This book or any portion thereof may not be reproduced or used in any manner whatsoever without the express written permission of the publisher except for the use of brief quotations in a book review.

First Printing, 2019

*Dedicated to Kimberly
and all my sweet friends
who have looked
the devil in the eye.*

Disclosures

This book is a memoir based on actual events. To protect the victims, locations, companies, and incidents may be modified, with fictitious names. Any resemblance to real people, living or dead, is purely coincidental and unintentional, since none of the persons in this book are real.

The author offers her own spiritual and legal perspectives on domestic abuse and the family court system. This book is not intended to give legal, psychological, or therapeutic advice, nor should it be used for that purpose. The author is not responsible for personal decisions based on the subject matter contained in this memoir. You are advised to seek professional assistance in your area as it relates to your particular judicial system.

This book is focused on spirituality, reproductive rights, and the effects of Narcissistic Personality Disorder on both males and females. No implication of gender isolation as it relates to NPD (Narcissistic Personality Disorder) is implied within these pages. Narcissists can be male or female.

Credits:
Editing: K.L. Walters
Contributions: Rabbi Jonathan Kligler, Woodstock, New York
(**www.rabbijonathankligler.com**)

Contact Info:
Jess Moravian
12645 Memorial Dr.
Suite F1 #349
Houston, TX. 77024
jessmoravian@gmail.com

Road to El Roi

Table of Contents

Introduction 6

Chapter 1: The Journey
The Odd Experience of Dying 8
Puzzling Behaviors and Red Flags 10
Ranting and Raging 12
Public Criticism 15
Admitting A Dark Secret 21
The Worthless I Knew 23
The Miracle Begins 30
The IRS 33
Strife and Sibling Hatred 35
Alone Again, Naturally 39
The Accident 43
An Investigation 47
A Kept Agreement 49
Popcorn Machine 54
"Mom, Dad Has New Guns!" 57
Out of the Starting Gate 59
Court Escapades 64
Bullying and Attorneys Who Don't Get It 71
My Church, My Shelter? 74
Tax My Ax 77
Second Field of Misery 80
DNA to the Rescue 85
El Roi Appears 89
The Telling 94
A New Case 98

Filing Complaints 108
The Retreat 112
Mean Church 115
Continued Antics 120
Destructive Women 122
Corruption in The Swamp 131
My Second Escape 136
Summation 138

Chapter 2: Spiritual Relevance

My Journey as a Handmaiden 140
Hagar by Rabbi Jonathan Kligler 142
Where in The World Is King Solomon? 150
The Isolation that Narcissistic Abuse Creates 157
Mean People and Busybodies 159
Flying Monkeys 161
Crazy Making 165
The Millstone 168
Church Alienation 170

Chapter 3: Exposing the Problem

78 Court Appearances and What? 176
Degrees of Pathology 178
Kids for Sale 181
Feeding the Monster 183
Children Defined as Property 186
The Doors: Family Court as Phony Theatre 189
Magic Eye 193
Banana in the Tailpipe (Parental Alienation as a Tool) 195

Chapter 4: Healing in The Maelstrom
Darkness vs. Light 199
Wait, Am I the Narcissist? 201
The Five Messages 205
Your Kids Won't See It the Same Way 214
The Girl in the Photo 218

RESOURCES

Readings That Soothe And Comfort 221
Children of the Gavel 226
Flowcharts of Narcissistic Identifiers 228
The Wisconsin Power Wheel 231
Recommended Books, Movies, and Blogs 232
Glossary of Common Terms 235
References 239

Introduction

I've rewritten this introduction more than a dozen times. I still feel inadequate, exposed, and off-center. The conviction of writing this memoir has held its grasp on me for the past several years. I still hurt from the sting of perhaps failing at least one of my children. Everyone who has grieved the loss of a child's affection or suffered at the hands of a falsified persecution in the family court system needs to hear from someone who has walked a similar path.

My hope is that this book will reach out to someone out there about to make a grave mistake in marrying or having a child with the wrong person, and that my story will cause some to realize that what they are experiencing is abuse.

Road to El Roi is a saga—a journey into Truth and in my case, a realization of the magnitude of detail that God is capable of handling. It is an exercise in being weak and imperfect, persecuted and despised, yet gloriously _seen_. The illumination I received while at a camp retreat formed the basis of my spiritual sisterhood with Hagar, the slave and surrogate mother for Abraham and his wife Sarai and made sense of the journey I'd been on for many years. I thank Rabbi Jonathan Kligler for his brave writing on Hagar.

Other victim stories are included within these pages, and I'm honored to know many strong souls who endure never-ending harassment at the hands of narcissists. When you go to war, you at least are consoled that your country and family are loyal to you and will celebrate your return. When you enter the epic battle of divorcing an abuser, you may suddenly find yourself estranged from and rejected by those you love; even your own children. There are very few in this world who know what it means to lose "more than everything." There are frail angels walking among us who know this condition too well. Imprisonment and separation can come in many forms, and many people aren't free in their lives.

We as survivors of this holocaust of hearts and minds need to know that we are understood, loved, and even admired. There is no message clearer to me as I've traveled this ugly road of court-sponsored abuse that atonement is coming for those who have carelessly discarded the rights of children, the respect of mothers, and the sanctity of Truth.

Shalom,

Jess

Chapter 1: The Journey

The Odd Experience of Dying

I was 25 years old and had been in a panic trying to do wedding details, and Chuck had been working out of town. It was about 4 weeks prior to the date, and the invitations had been ordered. I hadn't been able to get bridesmaid dresses in a timely manner. Details were blowing up, and I was fretting. Chuck and I were down to only one day together before he headed out of town. I said, "How are we going to get this done? What will we do?" I was in a semi-state; however, there was nothing directed at Chuck negatively in my question. There hadn't been an argument or even a hint of an argument coming.

The next thing I knew, I was pinned against a wall in my apartment with his hand pressed hard against my neck. I felt myself choking and struggling for air. The pressure of his grip compressed my windpipe. My brain began to whirl. "Would I die here?" "Was this it?" "What happened?" I hadn't had time to run or to get away. But I remember the feeling of suffocating, and my throat crushing.

Chuck whispered, deep, low, and raspy, "You're driving me crazy."

When he did finally release his grip, the good old transparent me (the girl I would learn to hide in years to come) announced, "I can't marry you," while choking back tears of devastation and shame. Why shame? He had choked me, and I felt shame? This is one of the mysteries of spousal abuse, of domestic abuse, and rape.

Chuck cried, he begged, he pleaded. He wouldn't ever do anything like that again. He hovered around me like a shadow the entire night and next day. He clung to me. Why didn't I wait until he left, call my family, check myself into a domestic violence shelter, and file a police report? I do know why now. It was because a) I'd never been educated on domestic abuse, for one, and b) I blamed <u>myself</u> because of a). Was I fearful he would kill me after breaking off the engagement? And the biggest WHY was: why didn't I stop and question his prior history of having a former fiancé break off an engagement just weeks before their wedding? He couldn't possibly survive another broken engagement -- yes, I felt sorry for him. It never even dawned on me that something scary might have happened to that girl, too.

Knowing what happened with the former fiancé might have held a treasure trove of information. However, I'm convinced that if I had broken the engagement off, something awful might have mysteriously happened to me. He couldn't afford another 'failed wedding' in his friend group he held so vitally important--it would have affected Chuck's image as an all-around great guy. However, as I found out much later, Chuck would have just made up something to make it my fault in the end, anyway.

Maybe I saved my own life that day by not breaking it off. I'll never know. This is why I refuse to criticize women who stay in abusive relationships. In many cases, staying with the abuser is the only reason they and their children are still alive.

Puzzling Behaviors and Red Flags

The wedding did happen, a few weeks later. It's amazing how you can mentally block a major event when you're trying to deny reality. However, it caught up with me; I got the full-blown flu on my honeymoon. I ran a high fever and could not sit up on the plane back. I was deathly ill, bedridden, and it lasted over 2 weeks. I still think my body was exhausted from trying to deal with the events that happened weeks prior. I had put on a brave face; a happy face. The show had to go on!

After I recovered, I saw a different person in Chuck. He slung condescending comments and developed a disapproving scowl that bewildered and humiliated me. It is as if a light switch threw after the wedding. A glaring, cold stare accompanied many reactions to anything I said, and I began walking on eggshells in my daily life.

It was as if a mask was lifted, and his true nature was revealed. Critical, distant, and unmoved, he became a person I had seen glimpses of prior, but now this was his dominant personality -- but only when he was alone with me. Most poignantly, he valued time with his high school friends more than our time alone. I liked his friends, but I'm an introvert; I've always needed down time. I was so tired I thought I might die. I began to wonder if my life would ever be happy. Chuck conveyed a completely different mannerism, personality, and persona when he was around others. His public self was in direct contrast with his private demeanor.

In effect, I felt as if I'd imposed on him no matter what I did. He never really seemed proud of me, or happy to be with me. He embodied a completely different "public" self when with his friends. I didn't understand it, and again, I thought it was all my fault for being so boring, so flawed, and just not up to speed with his friends' wives, who were perfect in his eyes.

Very early in our marriage, he lost his job in an acquisition and was without employment for a long time. We had to move in with his parents for a bit, and that started to really show his true mettle. I remember how depressed I was. He was always angry, but he hadn't started raging yet. Soon I would get acquainted with that new skill.

Ranting and Raging

Somewhere in our second to third year of marriage, Chuck developed a rage in which he would yell, march around, and point his finger in my face if I did or said anything he didn't like. I was bewildered as to what caused his outbursts. I began to read books to try and help me deal with what was becoming a difficult situation.

Of course, this became my problem to fix. There was a book called *Boundaries* by Dr. Henry Cloud, which helped me in some ways in dealing with the screaming episodes. I would announce to Chuck that if he continued his raging, that I would go to his sister's house to spend the night and that I would say why I was there. This worked temporarily to stave off his behavior once he realized that I might tell someone else.

This tactic didn't keep him in check for long. I began to notice that Chuck was always at war with someone, and if you were on the wrong side of that war, you were going to get lambasted. Chuck had, 2 jobs later, landed at a financial company. He always vilified whatever boss or upper management he had. Soon following the boss hatred was the church conflict. He'd managed to get himself involved in some committees and boards, and that had to center around conflict as well. It seemed that everything that touched him required confrontation and chaos. Female employees had a pattern of complaining about Chuck's verbal assaults.

During this time in our marriage, we also discovered that we could not have biological children together, and the reason given by the physician was that he was almost completely impotent, presumably from a childhood illness. Chuck had no motile sperm.

But how would we have children? I did want a family of my own. We could adopt from Russia, as a few of our friends were doing, but it cost tens of thousands of dollars. I was adopted in an interfamily situation that was difficult for me as a child. I didn't want to have my adopted child ripped from my arms by a biological parent who changed her mind.

New technologies offered some options, and so we embarked on a course of action to produce a baby. I won't go into details, but it involved a lot of money, a slew of tests, months upon months of procedures, and an incredible amount of stress and time. Those of you who have gone through fertility treatments know that it is not an easy trek. It is full of heartbreak, disappointment, and grief until things resolve.

Thinking back on how bad things were during those early years, I wonder why I did not try to escape this abusive situation? I have that answer, and those reading will already know why: fear. Fear that no one will understand. Fear that you're the one who is flawed. Fear of failure. Fear of starting over. Whatever the hesitation, just insert the word *fear* and you'll have the answer as to why victims stay.

As I've mentioned before, there is legitimate fear of death in overtly abusive relationships. As evidenced by numerous news reports and shocking domestic crimes, you can't always tell if someone will be likely to commit murder based on their prior behaviors. Frankly, at the time, it hadn't occurred to me that Chuck would try to kill me if I left. It seemed to me that he didn't want me at all.

Now that I know that in domestic situations, the further you are into an abusive relationship and you're weaker physically or financially, it becomes more about "trying to leave" than "leaving", as I found out years later. My exit from the marriage was a lot more perilous than I'd ever imagined. I'd never thought of myself as a possession, but rather a burden, and so I thought leaving would be easy and even welcomed by Chuck.

Public Criticism

In all of the stress of going through massive infertility treatments involving months of drugs, extraction of eggs, and procedures, I was emotionally spent, and fragile physically. There would be about 4-6 weeks of hopefulness and excitement, lots of meds, taking shots every single day until eggs grew, and then the main procedure. Then, you ladies who have gone through IVF know -- the days of waiting on pins and needles to take a pregnancy test was the most intensely stressful thing imaginable.

I would always lose my mind near the end of the cycle as time drew near to the pregnancy test to determine if the procedure was successful. That was when a pregnancy test might show results. I should have bought stock in pregnancy tests back then -- I bought so many. Cycle after cycle, to no avail, my tests were negative. I began to sink into a depression. What made it worse was Chuck's need to be social when I was in my deepest emotional gutter AND in pain physically.

I won't ever forget the time that on my third ICSI cycle, (ICSI is the procedure during the 90s which was performed using even non-motile sperm and inserting it into a live, cultivated egg in a lab, which is what we opted for at first) I was suffering from ovarian hyperstimulation syndrome (OHSS). I had no pain meds, and I was too stunned, disabled, and overwhelmed to even think of asking for any.

One of our church friends was having a birthday party and Chuck opted to leave me at home curled up in a ball. I don't remember having an arm around me, before or after he returned--a word of concern, a "how are you?" -- nothing. I'd been so conditioned to be ignored that I didn't protest because if I had, in addition to everything else I was going through, I'd have an angry, passive aggressive spouse who sulked, skulked, or gave me the silent treatment for days, maybe even weeks. I'd named it "the silent prison" and I was in it a lot.

There were in fact so many times that the battle had me so weakened that I didn't even try to leave, and couldn't think of exiting the marriage. Again, I blamed myself or that this was the station in life that God had given me, for whatever reason. It really went back to the same thinking that had caused me to marry him even though he'd choked me weeks before our wedding. I'd been raised in a fire and brimstone-type environment in which I was taught that once you made a commitment to a marriage, you were supposed to stay with it.

I really hate when people assume to know the mind of God, and then foist their assumptions on others whose lives are in the balance, constructing generalities about what 'should' be. I'm really careful now about what I say or even what I think when someone is going through relationship difficulty. Often, people with low emotional intelligence say what makes THEM more comfortable. They really can't visualize how a person they see at church and who serves on committees and donates money to worthy causes could be abusive. They'd rather think that it's something the other spouse is doing that justifies the negative behavior or the breakup. Life is really better when you are able to imagine that the people around you are all good people, and that there are reasonable causes for everything. As it applies to narcissism, those of us affected know that this could not be further from the truth. It is frustrating to witness the blindness of society regarding this insidious devil in our midst.

One of the other travesties to narcissistic abuse victims, especially female victims, is how the "good wives" will rally around a male friend of their husband's, and band against a woman who is being abhorrently treated, because the "good wives" will suffer if they do not. This is very sad, and I've seen it occur. It is a version of adult bullying.

Those who are active in the rallying around the narcissist are commonly tagged as "flying monkeys" (named for the monkeys unleashed by the wicked witch in the Wizard of Oz). She yells *"Release the Monkeys!"* and all hell breaks loose. Rather than the passive standers-by who do nothing, flying monkeys actually participate in the harassment of a victim. One of my friends going through narcissistic abuse has renamed the flying monkeys "friendlies" and "unfriendlies" as if there is a foxhole-trench-war going on at the middle school.

Outsiders really do not know at all what a person's life is like with any spouse. I know that my home life was in great contrast to the image I sought to project. However, Chuck still had a public history of screaming outbursts against whoever he was at war with at the time -- our minister, the church committee, his employer, or co-workers. It was always something; there had to be a fight. He despised his two sisters for most of our marriage. After the divorce, one became his court-funder and flying monkey. This is a classic pattern of what narcissists do; they cultivate the people they need.

What made things worse during this time is Chuck's propensity to take a social or church situation to criticize me in front of others. Once, we were out on a much-needed break, just a simple dinner out with friends. The wife was someone I truly loved. She is a gourmet cook and is paid really well as a high-level nurse. She has a close-knit, supportive family, and had been able to time her pregnancies easily, as there were no fertility problems affecting her and her husband. She's a really sweet person and was sensitive to my situation, and I respected her, which made the conversation even more embarrassing.

Just days after I'd been through one of the most traumatic processes in our attempts to have a child, at the dinner table of a restaurant, Chuck decided to announce that I never cooked -- as we were talking about Nellie's latest gourmet cooking feat. In reverence to her perfection as a cook, he decided to attack my home cooking. I was mortified. I felt absolutely useless in my life. It was humiliating but being the "tough girl" that I was, I chose not to react at the table, which would have made me look worse.

I don't really remember anyone else at the table reacting, either. I don't remember having a conversation with Nellie about it. I do remember Nellie conducting a Christian-based weight loss program at our church. At any rate, Chuck proceeded to go to her and proclaim that it was all my fault that he could not lose weight because I kept potato chips in our house. Nellie quickly told Chuck that indeed it was NOT my fault that HE could not lose weight. Nellie very much had the tendency to go along with the flow because she preferred peace, but she did not hesitate to call Chuck out when he said something crazy. For this, I will always appreciate her.

It didn't come to light until much later, when a male friend who was also in our Sunday School classes, remarked that the instances of public humiliation by Chuck directed at me used to stun him. It's so strange that no one called him out in public if so many people noticed it. It just validates how uncomfortable people generally are in confronting bad behavior. No one wants to get "sticky" in fighting back or have anyone be angry at them. It is sad that I did not seek help during this time. The situation would have been diagnosed easily by a competent counselor.

Remarkably, during one of our first failed IVF procedures, Chuck had met with some of his high school friends about our inability to conceive. I was not involved in the discussion. Suddenly, it was suggested that I go to a meeting with these friends because 'my mind must not be right' to not be able to become pregnant. Now, this is a man without sperm! What was being disclosed to these friends? Even as clueless as I was at the time, I believe I looked at him and said, "my MIND isn't right?" Chuck even involved our minister and his wife to drop off Bible verses to support our efforts. He later told another minister that aspirin had done the trick in creating my pregnancies.

Even I did not realize back then that as badly as I wanted children, he wanted them more. He had a problem, but the problem was him. What a dilemma for Chuck! No other female could fix this for him. What I was about to find out was one of the most hurtful things that ever happened in my marriage to Chuck.

Admitting A Dark Secret

I had gone through one of the worst drug regimens I'd ever been through that cycle. I think I'd eaten an actual whole chocolate cake in the process due to the insanely high hormone levels being raised in my body. I must add that it was a double-fudge sheet cake with chocolate buttercream icing, and I can still remember how it tasted.

It was near the weekend. Chuck frequently went fishing or hunting depending on the season, and he'd often be gone from Friday to Sunday. I never complained about it because I didn't want to be on his bad side, and he wasn't great company anyway. But I wondered sometimes if he could be considerate enough to let me know in advance that he was going so that I could make plans of my own. It was one of my most bitter peeves. Common courtesy is a cornerstone to my sense of civility. I would never inconvenience anyone by not notifying them that I'd be gone, especially if it was for days at a time.

It was regular routine for him. I'd know he was leaving when I saw his dirty duffel bag by the side door. That was always my notification. It left me angry and feeling disrespected, and this particular day, I was in no mood. I was looking at four walls alone all weekend, after spending weeks working alone staring at those same walls.

So, I protested. Firmly. I suppose I was trying to get some emotion out of him; something that made me feel like I mattered. After a blustering badminton game of volleyed words, I said, "I just need to know that you love me without kids."

Chuck immediately turned around with his back to me, did not say a word, grabbed his duffel, got in his jeep, and left.

I looked down at my keyboard at my desk, and knew then that there were deep-seated and probably unfixable problems in my marriage. I'd had a really hard childhood and really clung to the hope to have a family of my own. I had gone through weeks of meds; years of fertility treatment cycles and I was in my mid-thirties. I was in the middle of a cycle, having withstood the worst of it at that point.

I probably should have kept the fertility process going AND left Chuck. Clearly, I should have never married him after the choking incident. There were enough red flags besides that glaring one to sink a ship. But it is still clear to me that the children I ended up having were the children I was meant to have. I think that in a mysterious way that I'll never understand, God granted this unique option to me, and I've come to understand that my story has to be told.

Looking back on it now, I cried out to El Roi when I prayed while on a plane exactly to the day a year before Gray was born, "Please, help me resolve this issue with having children within the next year." I didn't know the yet the roller coaster of joys, victories, losses, heartaches, and miracles that would follow in the years to come. Also buried deep underneath was the knowledge that Chuck had made it clear to me that I was not loved. I was treading on quicksand, and in my youth and lack of education about emotional abuse, I was a broken vessel.

The Worthless I Knew

This struggle to have children during those seven years left me feeling worthless, even spiritually. Partially, it was the alienation I felt in my small community, and somewhat in my church family which seemed to focus on children and families. Looking at the situation now, I think it was also because Chuck made our inability to have children so public within our social circles. I felt as if I lived in a fishbowl.

He told his friends, he told the minister, and I just felt even more alone. I know now, after our discussion about whether he loved me without children, that this was IT for him. It was all there was; there was no *us*. I was told later in counseling by a clinical psychologist who understood narcissism, that Chuck treated me the way he did because our children were NOT biologically his. It was a condition of his physical deficiency for which I would pay the price for years and years, after attempting to escape the marriage.

Because of cost, the former procedures were no longer an option. Through an agreement with Chuck, I sought a sperm donor, and instead of sticking with the local donors to my area bank, I decided to branch out and look at every donor profile that was available in the U.S. I received fax after fax of profiles, along with their donor numbers. I had hundreds of donors to choose from. Finally, I narrowed it down to 2, and selected one that was most close to my side and Chuck's side of the family. I sent the fax over to Chuck at work. "This is fine," he said, with no emotion.

Why did I not think that reaction was strange? There wasn't even a real discussion; he did not come home and talk about the donor or bother to ask any questions.

Those really dark times that year in drug regimens and 2 more failed cycles left me feeling isolated, especially with my church. I remember that it felt good that Chuck would come have lunch with me in his city workplace during the days when I would have a procedure or ultrasound. I'd spend the rest of the day sitting at my desk alone working. I was happy, momentarily, just to have that company for one hour. I looked forward to simply ordering from a menu and being in a different place for a brief moment.

Once, I was sick from food poisoning after a procedure, ended up in the floor of the hallway of my house, and had to call a nurse friend to get some nausea medicine. During that time, Chuck continued to go hunting and fishing, continuing his habit of inviting his family over and disappearing until it was time for them to arrive, and not offering any monetary help to me during that time in which I was working sick, burning gas, and taking on more expenses back and forth to the city to get treatment. We did not have shared funds.

I'd read about the heparin recommendation for those women testing positive for an autoimmune condition which sometimes affects the ability to carry children (which I'd already tested positive for) and asked my doctor to go ahead and start me on it that next cycle. So, before the drug regimen even started, I was shooting heparin into my stomach twice a day. That was the cycle that I became pregnant. I won't ever forget the little line in the pregnancy test. It's interesting that I don't remember anything in detail about anything related to that announcement about Gray except that Chuck's mother Berna asked me if the baby was "ours." Her question really took me off guard, and I said, "Of course he's ours!" I'd decided to deal with that one later and I wasn't about to bust Berna's Catholic bubble or cause any angst for myself during this happy time. I was finally pregnant, and I knew somehow that the baby was a boy.

My elation lasted for weeks, but I had a lot of ovarian pain which I think was the remaining overstimulation from all the drugs, plus the insane amount of progesterone they put fertility patients on. Many, many ultrasounds to monitor development began at only about 5 weeks. Progesterone therapy continued, which served to really add some lovely bloating, and I became very, very sick. By 6 weeks, I was retching in the toilet, and that lasted for more than 20 weeks. But baby Gray was healthy in all ultrasounds. If not for grape popsicles, I would have been in the hospital with hyperemesis gravidarum (severe morning sickness requiring treatment or hospitalization).

I'd wait until the evening to take nausea medication, and then go to bed. That's how I spent weeks and weeks. After the emesis dissipated, I went on to gain 60 pounds! I'd been thin and fit most of my life, through diet and exercise. But I didn't care what happened to my weight, as long as the baby was healthy. Chuck continued his hunting and fishing trips, and I continued working, throwing up, and going to doctor visits.

Chuck, determined to be "fit" for the arrival of our son, went on to lose over 40 pounds and preen his body, exercising each day and dropping multiple sizes. He told people it was so that he'd be 'ready' for the baby. I cannot begin to express, ladies, how annoying this was! Once we were in a store and he pointed to me on the boxer shorts package that the thin, fit body in the picture is what he now looked like. He continued his all male get-away trips, and I spent a lot of time alone feeling Gray kick. We knew by then that indeed, the baby was a boy. I got wider and wider and my heparin shots were continued to the final weeks of pregnancy. Once I cut myself in a store and completely freaked out when the blood just kept coming.

During the last few weeks, when the doctors stopped the heparin, my blood pressure kept going up, up, and up and my ankles became little poufy pouches.

I knew that the Catholic Church disapproved of using donors. My Protestant friends were a more liberal group, but my circle back then might have looked at me as if I had a green head if I had volunteered the details of my conception. But I knew that God sent me Gray, because of that prayer I'd said a year prior on that plane.

I still (somewhat amusingly) think about how terrified I was about the reliability of the donor profile, but I didn't feel as if I could mention this to Chuck. Certainly, he would have dismissed the issue and scowled at me as if I was stupid. Since that fax had arrived in his office and I'd received the approving *"harrumph"* to proceed with the donor, that was the only communication he had uttered the entire time I'd been pregnant, about the issue. When I think back on that, I realize that I was afraid of displeasing Chuck by verbalizing my concerns.

Finally, after 18 hours of precipitous labor, more throwing up during that labor, and a C-section, Gray arrived. He had curly blonde hair and was navy-eyed, and he picked his head up in the delivery room as if he was going to walk down the hall or give a speech. I sat and cried when I held him, and that lasted for months. I was overjoyed. The first time a nurse brought him to me, she cried too. When I said to Gray in his little swaddle blanket, oblivious to the drama unfolding, "We waited a long time for you," my nurse completely lost it at my bedside. Some things, you just never forget.

On the first day I was alone with baby Gray, Chuck stayed at work for over 12 hours. I thought I was going to die from exhaustion. I felt so overwhelmed. I started working for clients 2 weeks after Gray was born. Chuck had stopped giving me the small "allowance" that I had been given for several years. That small extra stipend didn't buy a lot, but it had helped with groceries and household items. It's so strange that I don't remember asking him why. It probably wasn't worth the argument that might cause. Chuck made three times what I made. All I knew is that I had to get back to work. Gray sat sleeping in his baby seat while I did work for businesses.

Several months later, I was walking around with 5-month-old Gray, going about my business either working or feeding him. There was a sharp rap on the front door, which no one ever went to. I was served by a deputy at our home for an unpaid hospital bill which was being pursued by a local attorney. Chuck hadn't even arranged to pay the hospital for the child we'd waited 10 years for!

We had excellent insurance, and it's super easy to set up payment arrangements at the hospital -- all you have to do is contact their accounting department, and they set payments up. Instead, he'd hidden this from me, and my name was on the lawsuit too! Our baby is in hock, I thought! That was when I started to learn more about Chuck's financial irresponsibility.

About a week after Gray was born, Chuck joined a time-consuming committee at the church. I can't remember the name of the committee. All I know is that everyone was impressed that he had this new baby and that he was so willing to donate his time. What wasn't appreciated obviously is that someone (me) was at home alone covering 18-hour days, without any back-slapping accolades. He would come home after being gone 12 or 13 hours, eat his prepared meal, and announce he was leaving to go to a meeting. I had maybe 1 hour of waking time, the opportunity for adult conversation and recap of the day, before I would be faced with broken sleep, nursing, and changing, before it would start all over again. What I knew deep down was that Chuck would just about do anything to not spend time with me. It was far easier to be away and be praised by people in situations of outward importance.

You spouses who have had a similar narcissistic relationship know exactly what I'm talking about in the example above. As long as someone is looking, they are Mr. or Mrs. Perfect. Then they become their true selves at home. No one will believe you if you try talking about what your life is really like. For years, Chuck had even told me that I had no friends.

Our 10th anniversary was a few months later, after the birth of Gray. That anniversary, Chuck presented me with a bracelet of some value. I didn't really love it, but it was a great gesture -- until I read the note. In the letter, Chuck thanked me for providing him a son. I won't go into the exact words, but the result was -- here's real jewelry, since you've produced offspring for me. After having had the experience a year earlier when he refused to admit he loved me without children, I felt rather like a prized cow in an auction that had fetched a high bid price.

The Miracle Begins

Two years into Gray's life, I realized that since he was a donor child that he would likely never know any siblings (wow, was I wrong about that) and would forever be alone after we died. I realized we needed to find some way to provide him a sibling. I first started (because I just <u>knew</u> that our original donor wouldn't be available) by calling Catholic Charities about adopting a baby. We were unable financially to do a Russian adoption, which at the time cost over $20k and multiple plane trips overseas, and I was unwilling to go through the slow wait and risk of domestic adoption.

Catholic Charities had a program at the time whereby Korean children could be brought to the U.S. for an all-inclusive adoption fee. This enabled people not to have to leave the country (Gray was 2 years old) and still adopt; the children were brought to the U.S. I'd decided that this is what we could do—I certainly didn't care about ethnicity, and this was a viable way to welcome a new baby into our family.

But just before starting the paperwork, there was an instinctive nudge to my brain. As a last-ditch effort, I called the sperm bank and asked about our donor number (each donor is assigned an I.D. that the donor himself does not know at the time of donation) and any availability of that donor's sperm for a sibling. At the time, the donor material was more restricted, or rather, the sperm donation market was not as prolific. What the donor banks were supposed to do is restrict donors as to pregnancies, with fewer restrictions for additional siblings. It was highly unlikely that after 3 years, that there would be any donor (X) material available.

A person answered the phone at the clinic who seemed to be very knowledgeable. He said he would go check the inventory and I was on hold a long time, fully expecting to be told that there was no more donor (X). The man came back to the line and said, "This is really a fluke, because there should be no more availability of this donor, but there are somehow 5 vials in our cryo storage." I immediately thanked him, paid for the vials, and had them routed to my fertility clinic. A wave of shock hit me first, and then a joyous laughter. How great a sense of humor God has!

I now realize that God's hand was on me the whole time. It is amazing how slow we are to realize miracles are happening until something so amazing and complete hits us in the head enough to shock us into recognition.

I began the same treatment as before, starting heparin shots twice daily, low dose aspirin, and multiple trips to the clinic for ultrasounds. Weeks of hormone enhancing shots cost thousands, and the cycles (2 of them) cost approximately the same as the Korean adoption fee. I had no idea what I was going to do if the treatments failed.

The last cycle I was in, Gray and I got a horrible stomach flu, leaving us both bedridden for almost an entire week. I was running on empty. If not for red Gatorade, I might have never made it. I went to the procedure barely able to stand, but thinner than ever (BONUS). This is the cycle in which I became pregnant with Ren. I kept my pregnancy a secret that day until I could take Chuck to dinner to announce that we were pregnant again. I think I even paid the tab on dinner that night. I'd delivered again!

Chuck hadn't bothered to go to the procedure or even come home and keep Gray. I believe I had to ask Chuck's mother to do this. My awareness was there about his lack of consideration, but it had been so status quo for so long, it was part of my conditioning. I had already learned what putting up a fuss caused; further silent treatment. I remember there was a vase of roses by the side of the procedure table. This was my substitute for my husband being there when I conceived. How romantic!

Only if you've been through a narcissistic relationship do you completely understand how neglect feeds more neglect, and then you finally realize you are a frog in warm water. Before you know it, you're cooked!

The IRS

With Ren, I began my severe morning sickness a little later—at 8 weeks instead of 6. I'd learned to keep the nausea meds around, and I was now chasing a 2-year-old.

About a month before I was to deliver (I finally stopped throwing up with Ren at about 22 weeks) I was as big as a baby hippo even though I was watching my diet. I was peacefully working when I received a phone call from Chuck's workplace. He was subject, the office manager said, to backup withholding for not filing our taxes for over 3 years. He'd set up his paycheck not to withhold, and somehow the IRS had discovered there were no tax filings. Chuck had never mentioned he was doing this or communicated the issue in any way.

I'd left all the tax filing to Chuck because he had a CPA license and was his company's financial officer. Little did I know, he'd simply ignored the IRS.

Given his was our main income in the household, and here we were about to have another baby, I was mortified. In my usual "fixing" fashion, I decided that I would file the taxes. So, there I sat, Mrs. Baby Hippo, who could not pull herself all the way up to the table, filing 3 years of back taxes. It turns out all the tax returns filed were due refunds due to deductions and medical expenses.

My immediate concern was stopping his backup withholding, which I did, as soon as verification of those filings occurred. I also remember that there was not one question Chuck had for me, nor did he ever ask to even see the returns. I don't remember him thanking me or even acknowledging that I had fixed this large and looming problem. I think that is the first time I made a conscious "note to self" that something was <u>NOT</u> right with Chuck.

During the years leading up to this, I remembered that even related to his little longtime hunting camp he shared with friends, I'd overheard phone calls in which he owed just a few hundred dollars for the year and still hadn't paid. Then I remembered the mere few hundred dollars we'd been supposed to pay on a house that was rented to us at his old job. Turns out, he had never paid that rent either, for most of the time we lived there. Then there was the mortifying nonpayment of Gray's birth hospital bill. Did I see a pattern?

Strife and Sibling Hatred

One of the hallmarks of Chuck's family dynamic (with his siblings and parents) was that there was always some kind of strife or drama going on. He constantly complained about both his sisters, and usually I got drawn into the whole affair. Chuck said his niece was fat and she would never date, he criticized both brothers-in-law, and he constantly critiqued the whole family. The younger sister, Blythe, I was extremely close to and loved dearly. She had developed an alcohol dependency, but she'd been through a lot of grief in many areas—one of which was trying to have children herself. She felt like the outcast sister, and I felt like an outcast as well, so we got along great. She was funny and smart, and I loved her.

When I suddenly went into labor (3 weeks early) with Ren, I called Blythe first, before Chuck. This was in order to get my 2-year-old, Gray, to her before we went to the hospital. I could tell I was contracting, so I calmly called Chuck, told him I was headed to the hospital, and drove myself. This may sound strange, but I was really used to doing most everything alone. I honestly thought it would end up being a false alarm and that I would be sent home by the end of the day.

At the hospital, they put me on the monitors and determined that it was not a false alarm and that the contractions were getting stronger. My doctor had scheduled a C-section for 3 weeks later, but happened to be walking down the hall, and whisked himself into the room. Chuck made it to the hospital in time for the section, and without all the ugly throwing up during labor that I had with Gray, Ren was born. He was muscular and physical, and quite angry, turning beet red when being placed next to me in the delivery room. 3 weeks early, Ren weighed over 8 pounds! He had giant feet like a jack rabbit.

By the time my sister-in-law Blythe, who had Gray, made it to the hospital to see Ren, I was comfortably resting and attached to a pain drip. Gray was bouncing around like a normal 2-year-old. The only thing I really remember about the hospital visit is that Blythe smelled strongly of liquor. Her husband Dick was with her, so I made the assumption that Dick was driving. <u>*Of course*</u> Dick was driving, I thought; who would drive drinking with a 2-year-old to a hospital?

Thinking that I was being discreet, I leaned over to Chuck and said, "Please make sure that Dick is driving." Until a few days later, I never thought about it again. I knew that I'd have a sit down with Blythe about how we don't drink while driving children, and I know that conversation would be difficult but had to happen. Chuck could simply tell Blythe that Dick needed to drive, and we'd address the issue later.

What I didn't know while I was in the bed unable to get up, is that Chuck used the situation to triangulate a situation in the family. He'd called his mother, who was in her 70s, to report to her the "happening" of Blythe driving while drinking with Gray. He created a war within the family by attacking Blythe behind her back instead of privately addressing the issue with her. Who do you think ended up taking the family alienation hit? You guessed it -- <u>me</u>.

I came home barely able to move after the C-section and extremely anemic, and I didn't have any of my family around to help out due to distance. The entire family on his side was angry and upset. His father, Albert, took up for Blythe. His mother, Berna, was against Blythe. It had been turned into a feud. I don't believe Blythe and her sister Tabitha were ever the same again. This incident fueled the strife between Tabitha and Blythe. I was later told in therapy years later that Chuck thrived on conflict. If there wasn't some enemy to fight or malign, he was not happy.

At that exact time, while all that misery was going on, after I'd been home maybe a month, Chuck decided to be on the traveling minister-search committee at our church, along with starting *another* Master's degree. Both activities required out of town and out of state travel. This was in addition to working full time an hour away. I can't begin to describe the exhaustion of being alone with 2 babies day in, day out, and many nights. What's ironic is that the committee he was on took about a year to pick a minister, and Chuck spent the next 10 years complaining about the minister and trying to get rid of him!

Once, Chuck brought home a Christmas ornament from a trip and handed it to me in a clamshell case. It was very pretty, and I was excited to see it. It was late at night, and I was more tired than I realized, perhaps shaking from fatigue. I opened the clamshell, and the ornament tumbled onto the floor and shattered. The ornament breaking was in perfect alignment to how close I was to breaking physically and mentally. I will always remember this as a sad moment.

It would be months and months before Blythe and I had a chance to compare notes on what was said at the time of the family throw-down over her drinking alcohol while driving Gray. I divulged to her that I would have never gone to her mother to disclose what happened but would have confronted her face-to-face in private. I managed to save my friendship with Blythe after that, for a very long time, until narcissistic projection reared its ugly head again. I realized later that Chuck had actually hidden behind me for most of that time. He attacked his sister behind her back to their mom, and he didn't protect me from his family's onslaught.

I also found out after the incident that the day Ren was born, and Blythe was driving Gray, Chuck had followed Blythe all the way to the car at the hospital, and watched her drive away with Gray, and said not one word to her. It was more important to him to cause chaos by backstabbing Blythe than it was to protect to our son.

Alone Again, Naturally

Chuck ended up going into business for himself and raising money for a startup after leaving his employer. He worked long hours, which is ok in and of itself. I was never a needy sort, but it became extremely difficult to feel so alone. Once he drove over to the beach with us, sat and drank beer for 2 hours, and left because there was a non-vital meeting the next day that he wouldn't simply reschedule; I commonly had a sitter accompany me on vacation each year to help with the children. I needed companionship so badly. Once, Chuck decided to go with us, and I realized after I was better off alone – he started screaming at me in the car in front of our guests because he was frustrated at my not finding a restaurant fast enough. I didn't try to stop the "alone" vacations anymore after that.

I built flexibility into my work schedule to take care of Ren and Gray, who were now elementary school aged. I worked all hours of the day and night and struggled, but in my area no companies paid decent wages for my type of services. I had begged Chuck for years to give us a chance to move out of our depressed state to afford the boys greater opportunity. His field was easy to find work in.

Where we were, people paid large sums for private schools, because the public schools weren't regarded as academically sound. I had been a public-school kid, though, and had put myself through college with a job and financial aid. Chuck once said: "You didn't have a pot to piss in before you met me." That comment stuck. Chuck thought less of me because I put myself through school. Chuck looked down on me.

When a historical storm was threatening and it was time to evacuate, Chuck reached in his pocket and gave me $140 and decided he would stay home. I traveled alone hundreds of miles and spent 24 hours in a dark hotel room with only a cell phone light for illumination. I was terrified because even if you had cash, the gas pumps wouldn't work without electricity. I was hundreds of miles from home with young children and for the first time began to understand feeling like a refugee. I will always have a soft place in my heart for mothers wandering in strange lands with young children.

When I returned, traumatized but safe with Ren and Gray, it was weeks before we got electricity back. I continued working as hard as I could, but I was out thousands of dollars of lost business time and household expenses and was trying to stay in business. It was as if a bomb had gone off in our area economically. I continued to survive, but my frustrations within were growing. I couldn't overlook the fact that nothing ever changed with Chuck.

I tried to support Chuck wherever I could; it seemed he was always at war with his employers. There were screaming matches with his investors and hours-long board meetings, cancelled personal plans, and 100-hour weeks. Conflict seemed to surround Chuck at every level: work, church, and family strife. He brooded and stayed silent at home—many times I'd sit at the dinner table in which he said not one word the entire evening. There was a frown on his face all the time. Sometimes, I'd get up from the table from another silent dinner and say, "Nice talking to you."

I'm reluctant to talk about intimacy in this book because back then, intimacy paled in the face of larger issues. I am only mentioning this out of curiosity, as I'd like to hear from other victims. After the birth of Ren, I developed a chronic bladder infection that would only erupt after sex. My doctor claimed that it was a "structural change" after having children, and that I would need an antibiotic to take each time I had relations. I remember the physician prescribing a 30-day supply with no refill. When I ran out, I called the nurse and said, "Am I not allowed now to have sex more than 30 times in my life?" The nurses laughed and extended the prescription.

Chuck took no ownership of this situation, in the sense that if I would run out of the pills or if I got a bladder infection anyway, he would just shrug his shoulders. He never became proactive about this issue. I had wondered early on in the emotional state I was in that perhaps I had become allergic to him. His uncaring and flippant attitude about this worrisome physical burden in my life was another weight that tipped me over. I was in pain, and nauseous with each infection. I worried before and after each sexual encounter with Chuck.

What I do know, is that when I finally left Chuck, I never had a bladder infection again. There has been no evidence or hint of infection since. I no longer believe in the prior "structural change" diagnosis from my doctor. I believe now that my marriage to Chuck was literally making me sick.

Then Chuck's morose demeanor became even worse. I reached out to a friend who was a physician's wife who had treated Chuck for other issues. I remember calling her and asking if there was any way Dr. Paul could prescribe medication for Chuck's moodiness. I was blown (I was so naïve then) when she said, "Jess, doctors can't prescribe something for anybody but the patient." I must have sounded like a crazy person. I constantly Googled terms like, ***the angry spouse, the moody spouse***, and the ***silent husband***. I was at a total loss as to what to do.

The Accident

During one busy fall, I'd had an ominous feeling for weeks that I was going to be 'out' for a time period because of some event. An illness? I wasn't sure. It wasn't like I thought I was going to die, but it was the kind of inner urging like "go get a new nightgown". The feeling wouldn't leave me. It wasn't dramatic; just the impending feeling that I was about to be derailed. I'd passed it off as fatigue or over-worry. Nothing was happening, nothing had happened, and I felt fine. I was working hard handling political campaigns at the time. We'd just won an elected office that weekend. I had a meeting the next day to network with a larger firm to propose a partnership or alliance to grow my business.

Then it happened.

I was driving to pick up Ren and Gray from their school. I had just come from a client's office. Stopped behind a small vehicle turning left, I was tired and distracted, but I had my seat belt on. I wasn't looking in my rearview mirror. I was told by the nurses that this is the reason I wasn't hurt any worse.

Suddenly, it was as if I was strapped into a roller coaster seat and I had no idea how I got there. I heard myself screaming and there was a searing pain in the left side of my head with an audible "crack". When I came to, the car was still, and I could see the giant knot-ball coming out of the side of my head. I imagined that it was possibly my brains swelling up out of my skull, and I would die and never see Ren and Gray again.

I looked to my left, and I could see an elderly man in a big car, awake but not moving. I looked to my right, and my cell phone was on the passenger's seat. I reached for it and braced myself for not being able to remember any phone numbers (since my brains were still coming out of the side of my head). When I could remember Chuck's cell number, I realized that my brains must not be coming out of my head. *Folks, you just can't make this stuff up.*

Chuck did arrive in time for the ambulance arriving. It turns out, the elderly driver had hit me at 60 or 70 miles per hour and had never seen me. Both his legs were broken, and he died about a month later. I ended up with a concussion. Gratefully, the teenager who had been in the small car ahead of me had gone home unscathed because I was between her and that speeding hunk of heavy metal.

Always the efficient mom, I got home from the emergency room grateful and thinking that I was finally going to get a couple of days to clean out closets. Instead, every time I even tried to type on my computer keyboard, double letters were showing up on the screen. I was a copywriter. As it turned out, I would not write creative copy for months. I would not feel like myself creatively or energy-wise for one full year.

I fought my way to work after a few days, and would endure my days, taking a pain pill in the evenings. The searing headaches and sensitivity to light and noise were a constant drain on my energy. The first day I was home from the accident, Chuck stayed gone with Ren and Gray until late. I had no idea where they were.

I don't remember Chuck even coming home more than once to check on me. He'd called his mother Berna in to drive me to the insurance office.

My entire top part of my face was turning black, and I remember Chuck just looking at me and saying, "Wow." That was it. No hug, no arm around me, no kind words. When I was finally able to get in a car and ride, I was wearing giant sunglasses. When I removed them, it looked like I'd been beaten to a pulp. My car was totaled. My vehicle was a tank in comparison to most other cars on the road. The entire frame was bent, and all I could think of was that I was the luckiest person on the planet that Ren and Gray were not with me. The impact had pushed the back seat forward over a foot.

Any time car seats are in an accident, they must be replaced to ensure that they have full functionality. I was in the car with Chuck several days after the wreck, and I told him we needed to go a few miles out of town to buy new seats. I remember him being annoyed with this, but I ignored him. I was happy just to be out with the kids. When I put the new car seats up on the counter for checkout at the store, Chuck immediately put both hands in his pockets and walked away from the checkout line, with his back turned. I couldn't believe that he didn't even offer to pay for his own children's car seats! I was struggling to keep contractors paid, keep my head above water in a major crisis, and didn't even have access to his checking. I remember feeling abandoned.

A few weeks later, I was using every last dime of income trying to keep my business afloat, and I was completely out of cash to even eat lunch. I went by Chuck's place of business, in which he now was their chief executive officer, and uncomfortably told him I was hungry and asked him for some money. I have low blood sugar, which Chuck knew, I was shaking and still reeling from the concussion. I still remember how Chuck reluctantly shoved a folded $20 bill at me across his desk. He did not offer to take me to eat; he just pinched the money at me. If I'd been a beggar who came in off the street, the transaction would have looked no different. I felt as tall as an ant, like someone who was an annoyance or burden. I didn't know at that time, but there were things I couldn't have possibly conceived of going on inside that business with Chuck.

An Investigation

Chuck's conflicts with his employers continued to escalate after my car accident. He constantly canceled on plans involving the kids. Things were deteriorating. There was always a coup he was involved in to get rid of an officer or board member.

Blythe had been calling me about collectors calling her house, and about Chuck calling her and making up stories, and what she called "lying to everyone" – she said he was telling her one thing and telling others something else. I told her I had no idea, but that things were extremely stressful at home, and I had been dealing with his depression and silence.

Chuck called me again at the spur of the moment to tell me he couldn't take Ren and Gray to their practices one evening, and I was exasperated because I had little time and energy left and was still healing. You could still see dark rims under my eyes where the bruising hadn't gone away yet. Fortunately, I had a little money because a check had finally been issued that day by the insurance company related to the accident reimbursing me. Personally, this check would get me through the next months. I will always look at that check as God's hand protecting me during what would soon be a devastating turn of events. It would be the only feeling of safety I would have for a long time.

Chuck arrived home much later and marched into the bedroom. He announced to me that he was being investigated by his company and that he was being forced into being off for weeks. I was mortified. His explanation for why he was being investigated made no sense. I won't go into it but firing a founder over an item placed overnight into a wrong account sounded *off*. But that was his story.

Ultimately, Chuck was fired exactly two weeks later under a veil of secrecy. Years later, I was told by a former advisor of the business that he was taking money from individual accounts and depositing them into his account. I was told that his calling Blythe was for the purpose of borrowing the money he took, to give it back, with an agreement that nothing prosecutorial would be done.

Considering all that I'd been through with Chuck, I surely would have appreciated knowing what happened, because I would have exited the marriage immediately. Still to this day, I shudder to think what was really going on behind the scenes. Perhaps that explains the high value placed on lunch money I needed weeks prior, and Chuck's reluctance to buy the kids' car seats right after the accident. Maybe his accounts were frozen; I'll never know. But his pattern of financial irresponsibility would continue to terrorize my life for years.

It's interesting to me now how I didn't meander back in my mind to the unfiled tax issue back when I was pregnant with Ren, or the unpaid rent from years earlier, or the unpaid hospital bill from when Gray was born. You don't want to believe bad things are going on, or that someone is just wrong for you, and your brain has a way of blocking things when you can't face reality. I wanted my family to be happy, safe, and secure. I wanted Chuck to love me. I wanted my marriage to work. I definitely loved Chuck; but things were crumbling around me, and I was losing my footing.

A Kept Agreement

Chuck had two more job losses after the investigation and firing by his board. My loyalty to Chuck did not waver. During this period, though, Chuck seemed to care less and less about our relationship and didn't make any effort towards evaluating why he was now unemployed again. It was always someone else's fault. He consistently refused to move to another area to start over where the kids would have better schools, there was a lower cost of housing, and I would thrive professionally.

I am sad to say that I'd come to the point of being repulsed when laying in the bed next to him. You girls know that this is a special kind of hell. I haven't ever been able to have a physical relationship with anyone I'm not emotionally involved with, and I am definitely a monogamous type. When I'm not ok, I'm not ok. I was so devastated about the realization that my affection for Chuck was dissipating that I found myself in a sobbing heap near the boys' bedrooms on top of the stairs in the middle of the night. I knew things would never be the same.

Back when Chuck and I were engaged, we had a verbal agreement: If one of us wanted out, we would be up front about it and ask for a divorce so that neither of us ended up embarrassing each other. Being a stickler for agreements, and having a memory like an elephant, I went to Chuck with a straightforward request to separate. I said I needed time to think, and we needed to live apart to sort things out.

Chuck refused to leave, and I couldn't afford to financially. He suggested counseling, supposedly after talking to one of his friends, which I thought was the least I could do.

I went regularly to the counselor, whom he selected. I felt rather "set up". There was an obvious disconnect with the counselor, who I could tell assumed he was this normal, loving guy who was just faced with a wife who suddenly wanted a divorce. Chuck parroted everything she said. I don't believe you can make someone who really doesn't have affection for you to suddenly be in love with you. I did continue the counseling with him, up to the point that he became physically aggressive again.

At that point, I phoned the counselor and terminated the meetings. She agreed. In all, during that excess of 8 months it took to actually get OUT of the house, I reported Chuck to 3 different counselors. I continued to attempt to get Chuck to move out, pleading that I would take over the house note, and that we desperately needed a separation, but he refused and became even more angry. He wanted half my company; he wanted half the kids. Basically, he wanted "his half" of everything. This was consistent with the way Chuck saw everything—the scales had to be balanced.

Once, when the boys were at friend's homes, he cornered me in the bedroom, raging and pointing in my face. I got away from him and threatened to call the police. He backed off and I went and barely slept with one eye open on the couch. I still wish to this day that I'd started filing police reports during that time. But my attorneys advised against this. Why? Because women aren't believed when they report abuse when leaving a marriage.

Reporting abuse is a now recognized and proven way to lose custody of your kids. So many of us endure so much wrong to keep the peace, stay alive, or retain our relationships with our own kids. What a sad state of affairs we have in this country! I had one divorce attorney tell me that unless he was beating me on a regular basis in front of the kids, there was nothing that would ever be done.

Another time, we were trying to patch things up while on a beach vacation. My back was out, and Chuck knew it. It didn't happen that often, but when it did, I had to limp around and try to keep moving until my back slipped back into place. I was barely limping around and when I woke up in the morning, the pain was excruciating. It would improve during the day. I have a super high pain tolerance, and I knew eventually it would correct itself.

That day, I barely was able to walk out into the surf about 45 feet from the boys. Chuck came over and began pushing me down in the surf. Not just one little playful push -- holding me down in the surf with his strength. I was hurting and I couldn't get up, and I was getting water in my nose. I thought, "Is this how he kills me now?" I was gasping for air. I remember at least one of the kids was watching. I've always wondered what this looked like from a distance. Did it look like "Dad was playing"? Chuck had a smile on his face the whole time.

One morning during that same vacation, I was sitting up in the bed trying to decide to get up, and he grabbed my hips with both hands and jerked me sideways. I screamed in agony. Chuck shrugged his shoulders and said simply, "sorry" with a bit of a smirk. I think these little incidents were Chuck's way of getting back at me for causing him trouble in our marriage. Or maybe it goes back to the choking event prior to the wedding, in which Chuck had already demonstrated his capacity for physical abuse.

Near the end, about the time of his latest firing, he began stepping on the back of my heel as I was walking. He would grin widely when I would turn around and expect an apology. I wondered at what point he was going to stomp hard enough to break my foot. I started watching my back about then.

That's when my business attorney changed the beneficiary names on my life insurance policies so that there wouldn't be any further motivation to eliminate me from the picture. That seemed so foreign to me, but my attorney was concerned. When I moved out, I slept with mace in the bed with me for months. I will always remember this time in my life when I wasn't sure I would survive my exit.

The day he was fired again, at the very end of our living together, I'd just stepped off a plane, the house needed groceries, and Sally the hamster had escaped while I was gone. Chuck phoned me and told me he'd been fired and that he wanted to meet me at a very public local restaurant where a lot of people we knew congregated, to discuss things. I calmly told Chuck that I'd be glad to meet him at an adjoining town, because being visibly upset and reeling from a firing in a small town was not a good look for him. As volatile as he was, we did not need a public scene to deal with.

He refused to go to the other location. I lost contact with him that day for about 3 hours until I got home with grocery bags and a new hamster cage. By this time, I was a tired wreck. I began cooking, I put the hamster in her new cage, got the kids settled in, and finally got a bath. Then, I grabbed a book and got into bed to enjoy a few minutes of peace and quiet. I was just feeling calmer when Chuck barged into the bedroom holding my underwear that he'd rummaged out of the laundry room, claiming (insert disgusting words here) there was a residue in them. I won't repeat the words he used. I guess somehow, I had fit in during going to the grocery and buying the hamster cage, having wild sex in some hotel.

Now, I can really be a smartass sometimes, and when angry, I can go cool and just spit something out. I looked at Chuck and said, "Why don't you go take that and have it analyzed." I don't think Chuck liked my answer. He grabbed the covers, pulled them down, grabbed my pajama pants waist, pulled them down and inspected my private parts. I can't describe to you, even now, what that did to me. I think I said, "You are an abuser." I was so grossed out and personally violated, that I don't know if I was thinking at all.

I know that event was truly IT for me. Chuck was losing control of himself and I was scared of his next move. That's when I started making finite plans to get out of the house. Still, the attorneys did not want me to file a report, the reason being that to be believed, I needed visible bruising, a trip to the ER, or broken bones, or to be half dead. I remember thinking that I was trapped in a life that no one saw. I think the attorney thought that there was some huge asset base to split and the abuse could be used for bargaining. But Chuck didn't have any money that I knew of, or did he? Whatever it was, I didn't want it. I just wanted Ren and Gray, and I wanted OUT.

Popcorn Machine

I'm not sure if I ever told anyone about my popcorn machine and its role in my escape. A friend of mine funded me some cash, because Chuck was not sharing any household income. I remember stealing food out of my own pantry to have any food at one point.

I had managed to move into a rent house and create at least some personal space for myself (and beds for the children using a rental furniture company) during that very volatile period between leaving the house and filing for divorce. I had a few thousand in small bills stored under the little popcorn bags in a standing popcorn machine that the kids had given me for Christmas a few years prior.

That period, victims, is your most dangerous one. It hasn't really gotten out in the narcissist's social and work circles that you've left, and so if something happens to you, it can simply be an accident and then their reputation and "ownership" of you is intact. There were so many times I felt unsafe. I was told by my business attorney to notify Chuck that I'd changed the beneficiary in my life insurance policy. I didn't think he'd hurt the children because that was all he was in our marriage for, anyway. I was dumbfounded that he even cared that I left.

One night, I ended up in a hotel room in another town just because my instincts were blaring loudly. The kids were out at friend's homes and I'd remembered that was the last time he became physically threatening. He knew the kids weren't around. I called my sister in a panic, and she said, "If you have an element of fear that is bothering you right now, just go." I did. I drove 30 miles away and checked into a local Marriott. I'll never know what would have happened that night. The desk clerks must have been wondering what was going on because I showed up looking disheveled and distressed. That night is still the most miserable night I have ever spent in a hotel room. I felt crazy and that I was there for no reason. I was out $100 for what? It derailed my work, and I'd had to leave the dogs in the house. I was even worried about the dogs. I was truly afraid for my safety.

That night, I called his sister; the one who didn't really like me. Why I called her, I have no idea. I suppose it was to notify her that I was taking action if he continued to harass me. Then, the next day, I emailed him notification that I would no longer tolerate his aggression and that I'd phoned his sister about his past behavior. This was so that he would know that I'd told someone about his behavior, and I thought it might scare him off since he'd be under suspicion if something happened to me. I was quite confused about what to do, really. I have no idea what I was thinking, I was reeling so badly. I was trying to reach out for help since my attorneys did not want me to file police reports, since they would largely be ignored.

To make the kids feel emotionally safe, I'd announced that I needed more office space and storage space and that I'd rented this little house and they'd have a bed there. That seemed to work in keeping them calm and staving off any conversations which would have caused them more grief.

I still hadn't figured out how I would handle such a volatile situation since they were quite young. But I was afraid if I stayed any longer, they were going to see the police come to the house.

Weeks later in the process, my attorney managed to get his attorney to actually make Chuck fund me some community property money (we had no division of property at that point) and things got a little better for me. But days before the meeting with the attorneys to decide on property, he came up with a made-up contract outlining what I would get, and what I would not get, and tried to make me sign it before we met with our attorneys. I emailed my attorney about his sudden contract and she said that nothing he would make up or get me to sign would be legally binding.

I ended up donating that popcorn machine to my church youth group when I became a temporary youth director later that year. To my knowledge, it still sits there to this day and I will always fondly remember the popcorn machine hiding place. It saved me, and I felt blessed to turn it over so that it could bring joy to kids while they were enjoying fellowship at my church. No one knows to this day how poignant a role that inanimate object played in my march to safety and freedom. I will always have a love of popcorn machines.

"Mom, Dad Has New Guns!"

One of the most disturbing things I was confronted with while on the last few weeks of remaining in the family home, was discovering handguns in a bag in our bedroom under the television in a cabinet. These guns were very near where the boys would look for a video or game.

I'd gone to great lengths when the kids were born to gift Chuck, a lover of guns, with a locking gun cabinet. These handguns were out in spite of the available gun cabinet, and whether loaded or not, it wasn't responsible to have them in any open area with young children around.

When I discovered them, I removed and hid them, and brought them to my attorney. He deemed them quite dangerous and while not loaded, he pointed out to me that handguns only exist for one purpose—to kill.

Weeks passed, and I had moved out, and one day the boys got into my car and Gray proclaimed, "Mom, Dad got new guns." The way in which this was delivered indicated that this was a comment that had been directed by Chuck. I was infuriated that he would use the boys as a delivery mechanism to discuss something that was so dangerous and scary.

Back then, I thought in terms of what "should have happened" which would mean Chuck should have addressed his comment about the guns directly to me. He was a coward and a manipulator. What was he trying to say? Was this a threat to my life that he'd delivered through the boys? I still feel creepy and cold when thinking about this. It was meant to scare me.

I did not answer Gray, changing the subject to a happy topic like, "Let's go get ice cream!" because I did not want him to be in this discussion any further. It's amazing how crazy you can feel when you are going through a divorce with a manipulator. I would not feed the flames, which is what my wise attorney would call "going vanilla". Going vanilla only worked for a little while with Chuck. The true magnitude of Chuck's maniacal control issues and perpetual anger would soon some out. My attorney, quite experienced in family court, said to me, "Jess, this is how it's going to be. You're going to get a new car, and he's not going to like the color of the car. And he's going to sue you because he does not like the color, over and over. Just get ready, because him suing you will never stop!"

Now, I think I said "What!?" and really passed this comment off because **who** would commit such a stupid, crazy, and expensive action for no gain? What court would consider such a case about a car color? Little did I know was that the family court system would almost be that blind, and that was precisely the game that Chuck would play. I had no idea that this state of affairs would last upwards of ten years, until I almost had to forfeit everything I had to make it stop.

Out of The Starting Gate

Chuck and I managed to do a property settlement and custody agreement in our attorney's offices, without a judge present. I settled for a very minimal support, far below what it should have been, to keep my company he'd threatened to take half of and put the phony contracts to rest. We had about a 60/40 custody agreement in favor of me and I was beginning to feel like a human again outside the walls of his oppressive control. I would get my coffee each morning in my own kitchen, watch the sun rise, and thank God that I felt alive again.

Chuck's failing to cover his half of expenses started very early in our divorce process. At first, it was more about being late with support payments. I remember bargaining with him to pay portions of agreed-upon expenditures and having to constantly send communication by email to help catch him up. Within 6 months of our agreement, he completely stopped paying any support or following through on the community debt order he was supposed to pay.

I had started over in a different home, a rent home, with rental furniture, and barely walked away with the company I'd just started. I wasn't guaranteed a salary. I wasn't in a position to have the entire agreement reneged on. Because Chuck was a "financial professional" I'd naïvely maintained in my head that he would adhere to an agreement, especially since the boys' quality of life depended on it. I couldn't imagine him dropping the ball on so little since he made six figures at his new (and seventh) job.

Looking back on this, I still hadn't learned from his nonfiling of taxes back when I was pregnant with Ren, or his not paying the rent on our home, and his not arranging to pay Gray's hospital bill when he was born. I still didn't get it.

About that time, I was done with working 24/7 and having no one to talk to. I was lonely sitting at my desk day and night, and I simply wanted to be able to converse with an adult. I joined eHarmony, and laboriously took their long personality quiz. Almost immediately, I began to be contacted by "matches" and when they turned local, I felt so exposed that I decided to cancel the subscription. My finger was on the "cancel" button, but my hand stopped when I noticed a tiny town I recognized in the profile: Leaf Harbor. I hadn't seen that name in a really long time.

I'd lived in Leaf Harbor a few years in my young life and attended kindergarten there. It was in a neighboring state. Who was this guy? Tall drink of water with a dog on a hay bale? He didn't look like your average stalker. Besides, I wanted the scoop on Leaf Harbor. So, I messaged. It took a day to get a message back. To make a long and possibly boring story short, Cody and I messaged for roughly 8 weeks before we actually met in Leaf Harbor.

Our first date was the county fair and livestock auction over lemonades and funnel cakes. He was different from anybody I'd ever met. He wrote handwritten notes. He helped kids and charities. He thought of things that needed to be done before I did. I didn't know where 'we' were going, but it was a respectable relationship. He sent flowers, and was a total gentleman. Strangely, we had the same food in our kitchens. We both carried peanut butter crackers in our vehicles because our blood sugar was low. It's so romantic as to what things become important in a mate as you get older.

It was over a month before Cody was aware of Chuck's nonpayment of agreements, and it was only because he asked me about it. I didn't want my new friend taken aback by my own personal issues.

Being the up front, ethical guy he was, Cody jumped into gear and began helping me and the boys. He funded school supplies, he funded groceries, and most importantly, he funded their first Christmas after the divorce. Chuck, having already missed four full months of child support, a summer of camp expenses, and a complete civil violation of not paying off a debt agreement (leaving me with an additional monthly payment of over a thousand dollars that he'd supposed to have paid off), rendered me incapable of providing Christmas for Ren and Gray. Although Chuck obviously knew it was the holidays, there was not one single effort on his part to offer a few hundred dollars for Christmas gifts. Yet he had a girlfriend, was going out regularly, and making nearly six figures at his job.

I'll never forget the feeling on Christmas Day when Chuck rolled into the driveway with his girlfriend Madge, to pick up the boys, with his vehicle loaded with gifts for his family. I knew then in my heart that God had sent Cody to me to help me weather the storm that I was in. Gray and Ren at that point only knew that they were getting two Christmases, so off they went, happy as clams. I sat alone at home that Christmas Day, since Cody was caring for his ailing mom and other family members, but my heart was warmed because God (and Cody) had staved off a disaster for me.

Just prior to Christmas, before Chuck became aware of Cody, he was still doing things like following me in his truck as I was jogging, cursing at me. He barged into my home and ate the pizza I'd bought for the kids right after I had come home from the airport and was in my bedroom changing clothes. He'd shuffle across my kitchen and take drinks from my fridge.

One day, I'd even caught him standing in the middle of my bedroom. This scary incident was a turning point for me. Another night, he'd openly screamed at me during a basketball game in front of dozens of people. I don't know what the screaming was about to this day. All I knew is I was exhausted, and the "vanilla" approach my attorney suggested just wasn't working. He had blocked me with his vehicle while I was trying to drive out of my own driveway. I was still somewhat fearful he might try to kill me. An electrician working in my home once observed him pulling up to my mailbox and rifling through my mail. I still slept with mace in the bed.

Chuck had managed to get his attorney to put in a clause in our divorce agreement that allowed no overnight guests of the opposite sex in either home. I kept to this agreement; he did not. Making sure we had a spotless reputation with the boys and with the court was important to Cody and me. Cody and I had discussed that we might not make it in our relationship, under the conditions of our living apart and my having so many years of child rearing to go. He was incapable of moving since his ranch operation was in a fixed location; I was incapable of moving since it was almost unheard of in my state to get a relocation order unless you were getting beaten every day or had some kind of restraining order. But we'd decided that God had put us together for a reason.

We married a few months later in a civil courtroom next to a jail cell since the only judge in the county was there that day. We spent nothing; we had no honeymoon. I wore a regular dress that was old. We spent that night in my home with the boys. Chuck continued his nonpayment of support for a full 11 months before we filed for contempt. Ultimately the reason we filed is that in spite of Chuck not paying support, he was still trying to direct our activities and bully our lives. I'd reminded Chuck about his missed support, and not once did Chuck respond to my emails. When we finally did file, Chuck ran from the document server in his vehicle until he was finally tracked down in a retail store parking lot.

A few years later, Chuck would be married in a gala affair at my church, with wedding registries and Ren and Gray in tuxes. A European vacation would follow that. Chuck still hadn't paid Gray's sports fees or reimbursed me for his half of expenses. Even worse, he attempted to stop me from having the boys the night before Mother's Day, when he was on his way to his European honeymoon. I even had to get an attorney involved in that and pay professional fees to get the boys to my house after the wedding!

When he was with his fiancé, he maintained a completely different persona. He got very nervous whenever he thought she might talk to me alone. He'd walk over immediately if he saw us together.

Court Escapades

This marker would begin my new saga of Chuck's court harassment. Almost the moment after we finally collected a small portion of what was owed for child support, opting to gain a more favorable custody schedule for the boys, Chuck began working on his plans to take back control of Ren and Gray.

He'd also begun having his attorney send letters to my attorney complaining about sports or my lack of participation. The trouble was, it seemed like all Chuck cared about was his role in the boys' sports. What Chuck would do is sign (mainly Ren) up for sports, not ask me, and then not tell me when or where practices were. He withheld as much information as possible. When custody changed after his 11 months of ignoring support, he made sure he was assigned to be a volunteer "coach" on exactly the days that were my at home days with Ren and Gray. I refused to join this badly organized and dangerous team, which proved to be the right decision.

The problem was that he would triangulate the kids in his actions. He would tell mistruths about my "lack of cooperation". What that really meant is that he suddenly couldn't run our lives from sunup to midnight. Chuck would not disclose where practices or games were in order to render me helpless in participating, then he would have his attorneys write letters about my "lack of cooperation in sports." Chuck operated as a dictator, not a parent.

One of the most hurtful things that ever happened in all my years of escaping Chuck happened early on. After I'd said no to Ren joining a horribly run team that Chuck had misrepresented every detail on, Chuck had Ren so angry about my declining to let him join, that he slung a football into my chest in front of a throng of other parents, hurting my arm. After Ren threw the football at me, and as I was clearly shielding myself from the ball, Chuck smirked at me and walked away. None of the other men reacted; they just stared at me. I was humiliated and embarrassed. Ren was never corrected.

What little Ren didn't know is that Cody and I were taking all of the proceeds we collected from Chuck in unpaid support to finally give him the vacation that Chuck had reneged on for several summers. His participation on that team not only created an unhealthy balance against actual academics and family life, it prohibited any family travel, or much needed down time. It took us weeks to finally tell Ren.

The incident with the football illustrates how weak our society is with regards to abuse of mothers. Chuck had egged and pitted Ren to physically harm me. He'd used an innocent child to achieve his goal. What did Ren learn from that? To respect his mother? To not harm women?

I so wish my judge had witnessed this incident. As it turns out, unless you can get an eyewitness to describe something like this in court, no one is going to believe you; and most everyone, as my attorney said, gets amnesia when it comes to testifying in court. To complain would have brought likely negative effects to me, not to Chuck.

Once, Chuck wanted to send Gray to an all-boys Catholic high school 45 minutes away that had a very expensive tuition. The reason he wanted this was that he had attended a similar high school, and Chuck always had a snobbery about public schools. The reality was that I had just been through a year of nonsupport, and we had barely collected what it cost to file. I'd finally settled into a home and had the boys on a reasonable schedule.

Ren was still young; how was our 2 hours in the road for Gray just to go to a status school going to affect him? I couldn't afford to move again to another city. It was also yet another 30 minutes further from Cody. We had already given up so much just for peace. This would completely blow up our family life. I knew Chuck would further use the out-of-town situation to further control Gray, and then he'd try to force me to send Ren to the same school.

Chuck had just been held in contempt a few months earlier for being unwilling to pay a small support payment, and now was suddenly able to pay for an elite high school plus athletic expenses. Chuck invited me to the school Open House. I had not been informed nor allowed to participate in any application process related to the school. My address had been misrepresented in all the paperwork Chuck created. He paraded Gray around, and when I got there, he did not speak to me, introduce me to anyone, or otherwise act like I existed. I was still reeling from the ordeal of court, being harassed left and right, and PTSD from not knowing what was coming from Chuck at any moment.

However, there was a happy medium available. An up-and-coming Catholic school 15 minutes away that had the status Chuck sought, had just opened with new buildings, respectable staff, and good resources. I stood my ground on the impracticality and cost of the distant school which often took over an hour in traffic to get to, not to mention the equally long ride back. Chuck and I had agreed on the alternate, closer school in a dinner meeting, and Chuck signed the contract agreement with the closer school. Gray had gone to their testing and scored the highest in the array of freshmen on their entry exam. I still remember leaving this meeting feeling overjoyed and telling Cody that we were going to have an agreement on this school. I was giddy. I should have known by the grin on Chuck's face when he left our dinner that he was up to no good.

Within one week, I had a court filing delivered to me by my attorney, with Chuck attempting to force me to send Gray to the out of town elite school. I later learned that he'd applied Gray without my knowledge to the other school.

He'd also talked Gray into collaborating with his plan. He'd convinced Gray that this was THE school to go to, and convinced him he'd handle things with me, and for Gray not to speak to me about the issue. This was my first experience in feeling alienated from my child. Now, Gray was just a kid, and Gray didn't know or understand the moving parts in our lives or the reasoning I had for objecting to the school. Any normal parents, even under disagreement, would have had a round table discussing the pros and cons of such a financial and time sacrifice for a far-reaching school choice with their child, then take on a unified front. Yet never in the discussions with Chuck was there any mention of carpooling, collaboration, or finances. There was no discussion at all -- only Chuck's dictatorship and court actions.

As a habit, Chuck regularly disappeared with the boys and ignored the clock. He forever threw monkey wrenches into plans with spontaneous sporting events; he checked the children out of school to gain more custody and do hunting trips. He lied and misrepresented my life to others. He made it almost impossible for me to work poor Cody into their lives at all. But the reality is, any time you lodged a complaint, it cost thousands to get it heard, and even if you got enforcement, the Chucks of the world would just look for another thing to violate. The whole thing becomes like a Whack-A-Mole game in an arcade.

I'd gone into defense mode. But I was devastated on the inside that Chuck had driven a wedge in between Gray and me. I'd forgiven Ren the minute he hurled the ball at me because I knew that all of it occurred under false pretexts. But it still hurt me to my core.

I'd been at Cody's ranch for the weekend, crying my eyes out while we fed cows, and when I got inside, I emailed the priest in charge of admissions at the school. I'd resigned myself to at least educate myself on what was truly going on, since I hadn't even seen the application related to the school. Chuck had already prevented me from getting mail from the agreed-upon school by falsifying my address.

I asked the priest about Gray's admission, telling him that I was having a hard time with the location of the school for our daily lives, but that I knew any school would be lucky to have Gray as a student.

It was a very respectful correspondence. The priest's reply, which came the next morning, was shocking: **Gray wasn't even admitted to the school, nor was he going to be.**

The priest went on to reveal that Chuck hadn't brought Gray to the required testing which was on a specific weekend. The referenced weekend for the test date had been on Chuck's weekend. It turned out Chuck hadn't bothered to do his own homework on the requirements of admission. But this time, he'd already involved the emotions of a child and also filed a very expensive case on an issue that wasn't even relevant since Gray would not be admitted.

Here is where I disagree with attorneys and I hope anyone reading this who sees a correlation in their own case, heeds my warning: my attorney did not want me to immediately show Gray the contents of the priest's letter, for fear that the letter wasn't accurate or that the judge would somehow overrule.

The priest had already stated in his letter that the school could not be forced to admit a student. But there was something wrong to me as a parent about withholding that letter that challenged my personal ethics barometer. In effect, I was playing a role in prolonging the delusion for Gray that he was getting in the school. And Chuck was still telling him he would go to the school.

If I visited this issue again, I'd have politely told my attorney that it was against my sense of right and wrong to withhold vital information that was affecting my child. It would be weeks before the letter was released to Chuck's attorney. I showed the letter to Gray as soon as I possibly could.

It even came out later that the school we'd actually agreed on had sent an award letter declaring Gray an almost full tuition scholarship because of his test scores, and Chuck had hidden the letter from Gray and me. Of course, he'd been able to do that since he'd had my address falsified and his as the custodial address. Chuck had hidden Gray's own achievement from him!

Honestly, this chapter upset me to write, and the stress of what I went through is still palpable. I remember going out on my porch and simply wailing, so loudly that the neighbors probably could hear me, from the pain of emotional and communication separation in my relationship with Gray. I shudder to think what could have happened if I had not been able to gain counseling for Ren, Gray, and myself. The events that began early in the court saga made me start to realize the level of dysfunction and (depressingly) the likely years I'd be going through subject to Chuck's dysfunction. What began to ring true to me was my attorney's assertion about the car that she'd made almost two years earlier.

Bullying and Attorneys Who Don't Get It

About this time, Ren, at about age 10, began saying things I didn't understand. He would say, "I have to kill myself if my mother buys me baseball cleats" and "I have to kill myself if my mother gets me a haircut". He would say these things randomly. I found this dumbfounding and mentioned it to the assistant attorney working on the high school case. They became worried, and within just a few weeks, there was a judicial court order for counseling for both Ren and Gray, and separate therapeutic counseling for Chuck and me.

What I know now is that Ren was absorbing the anger Chuck projected because of his hatred of me. This would come into play whenever Chuck's obsessive need for control got threatened. Crazily, a haircut or a pair of shoes were a threat to Chuck if I bought them for Ren.

A few times, I was witness to Chuck screaming at Ren on the phone about practicing or hitting balls; it almost always seemed to be about sports. Ren had been publicly humiliated in front of his schoolmates when he was wearing his favorite hi-top tennis shoes, when Chuck threw them across the school driveway, calling them a racial name. Ren had many friends of all ethnicities. Chuck just didn't care who he hurt when he was angry--even a child.

Gray got counseling about his anger with me for fighting the expensive and far away all-boy school choice, and Ren got counseling on dealing with Chuck's anger. The end result was that thousands of Cody's hard-earned money went down the drain for getting nothing accomplished but two kids who now needed counseling. But Ren especially had needed counseling for a long time. One of the things Cody was able to do with Ren, as a stepdad, was to teach Ren that screaming and yelling at children is wrong.

While the order for Chuck and me to receive counseling was still standing, I just wasn't ready yet to be in a room with Chuck. One of the things I'd like to change most about the system is when someone has been abusive to you, you really shouldn't have to be in close proximity to them. This is one of the mysteries of how our judicial system handles domestic abuse. If you have children, you have double-jeopardy (an abuser in family court can file on anything, over and over) and you are stuck with a lifetime of contact with your personal stalker.

It seems that in the courts, it's viewed as passable that we endure spousal harassment because it is our lot in life as women. The truth is, if a spouse ever hates you enough to hurt you, they will try to hurt you using your children. This has been proven over and over in news of murder-suicides, child-killings, court stalking, and permanently damaged lives. All you have to do is pick up a newspaper or view social media any given day.

I remember poignantly during one of our court battles, getting called into my attorney's (one of the ones who had no clue about narcissism) office and was told how disappointed he was to hear that Gray now wanted to live with Chuck. I just sat there frozen in my chair and thought, "Aren't you supposed to be working for *me*?" In tears and falling apart, I went to pick up Gray from practice. When he got in the car, I said, "So, I'm hearing now you want to live with your dad?"

Gray seemed just as surprised as me and his pupils were really large and wide open. He claimed he knew nothing about what I was talking about. I sat him down at home and calmly said, "Now, you are old enough to decide who you would like to live with, and no one has to go to court over that. If you want to mainly live at your dad's house, I'm not going to fight you on that." Gray said, "Mom, I never said that, I don't want that, and I do not know where that came from." I gave Gray every easy 'out' possible. The assertion I had gone through hell and back over that day had no basis in fact.

In the end, we spent legal fees deflecting this phony blackmail effort and had to go through stress over this attorney not even understanding that he was being bullied by the other side. Chuck had represented this to his attorney, and it got transmitted to me through mine. The scary thing is that this same attorney is now a family court judge. I hope he has learned more than he knew then, for everyone's sake.

My Church, My Shelter?

One of the striking things about Chuck, is that one day he could file false claims about me in court, the next day he could be in a room screaming and yelling at someone else, and the next day after that, depending on who you were or where you fit into his scheme, he was someone you would not even recognize: a charming character who is laughing, making jokes, and appearing to be an all-around great guy.

Chuck phoned me while I was at Cody's ranch to tell me he was getting married. I really wasn't sure why Chuck called me about this at night. Maybe he was looking for some reaction from me, but I was very glad to be away from Chuck forever; he'd turned out to be even more of a monster than I'd ever imagined. I told him I was very happy for him and congratulations. He went on and on about how the boys were very excited about the engagement.

Almost immediately, Chuck began planning parties, did wedding registrations, and planned a formal wedding. It was as if he was getting married for the first time. My church of 20+ years that I was active in was his choice of venue for the wedding. While I found a large wedding to be in questionable taste for someone who had been married for 22 years with 2 almost-teenagers, it was totally within his right to have a big event, if that's what they both wanted. I knew that Chuck loved attention and being the focus, and this is a free country, so Chuck could get married wherever and however he wanted to.

Chuck wasn't very active in our church at the time of my exit. He'd rotated off all serving capacities. But there emerged a clear pattern: when he was about to file a case against me, he amped it up and started showing up for any and every church event with Ren and Gray. I'll be honest: it did hurt me deeply when my church hosted Chuck's wedding **while** he was harassing me and in financial default.

I think while Chuck wasn't paying his share of expenses or making support payments, he was giving money to the church. Much later, he'd even refused to refund to me his share of a youth camp expense that I'd had to pay on Ren's behalf, insisting on giving the funds to the church directly so that he'd have a receipt of his "donation". That money went to his ego and external image instead of a bag of groceries for my household that was desperately needed.

During those dark times, my church was sometimes my only place of solace. I would have never made a big production out of my own remarriage anyway. I don't really see churches the same anymore; they are sometimes only groups people create who are struggling along like the rest of us. I think churches need to take a stand against violence and harassment, social bullying, gossip, and church alienation.

The church needs to be more cautious about being silent in the face of abuse because they are ostracizing those who need support. I think this comes under the category of the parable of *"throwing pearls before swine"*. A church with no moral courage is one that will eventually see its undoing. Imagine if, during the Holocaust, all religious organizations of power at the time had boldly sheltered the Jews and exposed their mass murders? Holocausts are going on all around us and are not mere fodder for history. The holocaust of family court abuse is ruining countless lives and generations of families.

I'm going to say something really controversial. I'm not even sure how I view marriage after my stint with the family court system. I know now that the minute you divorce that any children you have suddenly become "property" to be divided. If you are unlucky enough have been married to one of these vindictive souls, you may find yourself at risk of losing everything and everyone you care about. The narcissist's mantra, with the support of the "one size fits all" family court system, is: "How dare you leave me! I'll make you pay."

Tax My Ax

A few years after my divorce from Chuck, I was contacted by the state revenue department over a franchise tax filing that did not apply to our organization. While proving this and getting the issue corrected, I asked about my own personal tax account. I was told I owed thousands on a return that was never filed from a prior year. The actual bill on the taxes was assigned to Chuck, the primary filer.

Of course, I was upset, because I am a bit OCD when it comes to getting things straight, and I went immediately into my tax files. I could not find the return in question, and so I requested that year's filing copy from the IRS by submitting a form. When it arrived, I was shocked to find a huge income for that year on the return. This was the year that I'd had my accident, the year that Chuck had walked away from the counter at buying new car seats, and the year I'd begged for lunch money. The immediate next year was when he was fired under suspicious circumstances from his job.

My signature on the return was fraudulent. It was clearly not mine. Chuck had hidden this return from me. Where did the money go? What more did I not know about his firing from his company? This year was the absolute worst financial year that I'd ever had with Chuck, and here was a return that showed an income of double what I thought Chuck made.

I called my accountant, and he called the state. We found that Chuck had been ignoring notices from the state revenue department, and his hunting license had already been revoked, and his driver's license was about to be revoked. This would have been useful information to know while we were in a deposition with Chuck in which he was trying to prevent Cody from ever driving Ren and Gray. I remember my attorney asking Chuck in a deposition during his crazy high school case, about who he would consider a responsible driver; would it be someone with a valid driver's license?

One of Chuck's best hunting friends was a wildlife officer at a high level in our state. After finding out about the revoked hunting license, I guessed that Chuck was simply running around with Brad and got away with not having a license that way. No one was going to question or stop Brad if they were out hunting or fishing together.

Chuck had established a clear pattern of ignoring authority and of financial irresponsibility. I later found out that he'd almost lost our house (which he demanded to keep or he'd take half my company) after we separated due to a tax issue; the same house that I'd begged him to simply let me take the note over on so the children wouldn't have to leave their rooms. I found out he'd borrowed even more money from Blythe, and possibly from his other sister Tabitha, but it's anybody's guess what the story was to them. All he had to do was make sure I was alienated enough so that they never talked to me. I can almost guarantee that Chuck's story was that I caused the problem.

In a later statement, not knowing that I had all the paperwork to prove that my signature had been forged, Chuck claimed in a deposition that the entire issue was caused because I had not filed out taxes that year! He'd then used the excuse that his insurance agent had caught the fact that he had no driver's license. I had copies of the multiple notices that had gone to Chuck's home address.

But in all his statements, even under oath, he claimed that I had not filed those taxes that year. Chuck just couldn't stop lying. I can't even list the number of times I had proof of just the opposite, and amusingly watched Chuck spin his tale. He'd even lie when there was no reason or benefit to him for doing so.

I breathed a sigh of relief at not being associated with Chuck businesswise anymore, but it still shocked me, even then, to discover even more of the chronic nature of his pathology. Around that time, I discovered Tina Swithin's book *Divorcing A Narcissist*, which is a must-read for anyone going through a divorce with a vengeful ex.

In *Divorcing A Narcissist*, Tina details all the tax antics of her then-husband, Seth. In the book, Seth exercises complete financial destruction, ignoring all taxing authorities, and loses the family home to the IRS, which freezes all their accounts. Swithin is left with nothing, entering a shelter with her two young daughters. Her story was so similar to mine that I remember sitting up in bed with a highlighter and ending up with an almost entirely neon yellow book. I was thrilled to be no longer alone in my wandering through this confusing place that I had to raise children in. It was a shocking discovery for me as to the pattern of behaviors in individuals with Narcissistic Personality Disorder (NPD).

Second Field of Misery

Less than a year after the orders for custody, when I thought things might be getting better for Ren, there was a systemic failure in more than one area: Chuck, while paying support, was not reimbursing for clothing expenses, sports expenses, and he'd even failed to pay a basic school fee which caused Gray to be called into the office at school. Chuck was still blustering around trying to control everything, but since he was in wedding mode with all his festivities, I got to keep the kids a lot, which worked great for me. I think that his new fiancé had no idea of his long history with the court system before their wedding. Chuck could maintain a completely different persona for a very long time.

During that year, Ren had been increasingly asking not to have to go to Chuck's house, and I was super upset about the stress level I was seeing in him. Even when Ren would ask if he could stay at home with me when he knew Chuck was going out anyway, Chuck would refuse him. While Ren had asked to see the original counselor a few times and then said that things had improved, it was always only a few months before Chuck was right back to his raging.

Ren ended up back at the psychologist's office and I sat in the waiting room, thinking that I might never know what was said. It was then that the psychologist called me in, to a sobbing Ren. Ren had disclosed that Chuck would wait until no one was around to scream and yell, and Ren was having great difficulty coping. I was just dumbfounded that this was happening again; I did not see it coming. I'd always thought that he went after Ren because it was harder to get Ren to turn against me than Gray. Then I decided that

Ren was more like me, and that angered Chuck. My biggest concern was that Ren took my place as the emotional punching bag. Gray had a skilled political tactic with Chuck and had learned how to navigate around his eccentricities to a great extent. Ren was just Ren 100% of the time, and he was sensitive and empathetic.

That was when I began urging Chuck to participate in counseling again. But he refused. He also continued reneging on shared expenses. I had changed attorneys, which I think to this day was a big mistake. Those of you in this road to indignity know that along the way, sometimes you start feeling like your attorneys don't want to represent you, don't understand you, or become impatient with your situation. It also turns out that many court orders do not enforce things such as refusal to reimburse agreed-upon expenses.

With crafty lawyering, sometimes only the strict child support is enforceable, while the larger portion of what is not being met, is "soft" and with no accountability demanded by the particular court system you're in. That is when you truly begin to be aware of the "game" of family court. Attorneys, even good ones, can't always protect you "in the event of a narcissist".

This was my situation with Chuck. He had managed to find out exactly what he could get away with and was doing it. As to Ren's situation, by the fall of that year, I had a letter from the clinical psychologist, and an agreement from another (court appointed) psychologist with a recommendation that Chuck NOT have any more visitation with Ren and possibly Gray until the court was able to enforce the counseling order and the issues with Ren were properly addressed.

I remember waking up that next morning after receiving the report, not believing that I had been finally validated by a professional about what was going on with Ren. I had been praying daily for Ren and Gray, and it was the only thing during those hard times that kept me upright and using complete sentences. I felt so absolutely alone; Cody and I still could not live together as he was still having to run the ranch, and I was becoming more and more alienated by the constant drag emotionally and financially of the court battles. I was still expected to collaborate with Chuck on sports and events involving the children. To be an effective parent and to go "along" with court orders, I had to continue to make the effort yet still be around this person who had abused me and was now intentionally trying to wreck my life.

Another event that was happening that year is that I was losing my judge because of redistricting. The newly elected judge, I knew nothing about, but my attorney assured me that "he'd gone to school with this guy" and that we probably stood a better chance with the new judge to get something done about Chuck's bullying. My instincts were blaring loudly during this whole process, and I felt strongly that I needed to get in front of my old judge, who had always treated us fairly and knew Chuck's history of violating his orders.

The very last available date that my previous judge had was the Monday after Thanksgiving, and I scheduled my hearing, with the psychologist testifying. Chuck threatened through his attorney to drag Gray and Ren into court and put them on the stand. My attorney phoned me and said to expect that, and that he did not expect good things, because he thought the judge would be annoyed at us asking for a special hearing. The threat of Ren and Gray being dragged by Chuck to court, further traumatizing them, was too much for me as a mother. Chuck and his attorney likely knew that I would not add further harassment of the children to the mix. Tearfully, I called my attorney and asked that he continue the hearing and it would roll over to the new judge that my attorney was so crazy about.

To this day, I still think this continuance and client pressure was more about two attorneys not wanting to have to try a case the Monday after Thanksgiving. The bonus was that I peacefully was able to enjoy my children and Cody's family that holiday. On that Monday, I dressed for court and went alone in a peaceful protest and honor of my judge, who kept quizzically looking at me and even asked out loud if there were any more cases to hear. That day I watched another case unfold in family court, in which a young attorney tried to represent that a father should be given domiciliary control of an 18-month-old for no stated reason except that the mother had moved out of the home.

I looked at the father as their case went on, who appeared awkward in his suit, shifting from one foot to another, and wondered if the conservatively dressed young mother on the other side of the room with her attorney had been physically assaulted. What was the back story? It would certainly never come out here. I watched as the dad had his family members in the courtroom glaring at the mom, who was alone. I felt sad for her. That day's fight was over Christmas, and I remember the judge splitting the days she would see her child. My earnest hope is that this mom is not in this war anymore, and that her daughter is ok.

Part of the agreement in continuing our case that day was that Chuck would agree go to counseling. I naïvely was consoled by this and my attorney's words that the new judge would be excellent. I asked my attorney specifically if the prior judge's order for counseling would be honored, and my attorney told me that since the order was in a judgement, it would not change. I had no idea how terrible this piece of advice was.

DNA to The Rescue

During the latter part of the year, the same year in which the psychologist's report on Ren came out, I began to feel strongly that the boys' DNA and their status as donor children was becoming an issue. Ren and Gray did not know they were from a donor, and this was a failure of both Chuck and me in parenting. They should have known since they were young that they might have half-siblings. Gray had grown very tall and was taking on qualities that looked nothing like Chuck. He was also an academic scholar and budding scientist, and he existed on pure curiosity. It was only a matter of time before it became obvious. Little did I know, it already was. Ren was a little too young to suspect anything yet.

23andme (www.23andme.com) had just come to the forefront of DNA home testing. I had contacted Chuck by email multiple times about following the counseling order. I then emailed Chuck about the issue of talking about Gray and Ren's biological heritage in counseling, as it was getting to be time that we needed to do that, since they couldn't go through their whole lives not knowing where they came from.

Gray, Ren, and I sent our spit kits to the lab, and it took roughly 6 weeks to get results. All kinds of neat things emerged: Ren and Gray were 25% Scandinavian, which was no surprise since I knew their donor was Swedish. The bigger surprise, even to me, is that we were all of some African American heritage. The test revealed that my grandmother on my biological father's side had been 10% West African! The DNA maps were fascinating and showed the genetic history of our ancestors moving across the continents. I was adopted and never got to know much about my biological mother's ancestors.

I remember Gray getting very nervous as the test results were about to be downloaded. He said to me, "I hope it says I'm German." I replied, "I don't think you're German." Then I found out that Chuck had been telling the boys that they were of German descent. Chuck's family was almost completely German. Not only was he not sharing their true story, he was making up a false one for them. This is when the clinical psychologist got involved heavily in asserting that the boys needed to be told about their donor status as soon as possible.

There is an organization that helps donor children find their genetic families, and one of the founders wrote a book on how to tell a child he or she is donor conceived. Not only do donor children from anonymous egg or sperm donation have a real risk of dating their own half-siblings, but the later they find out that they have been lied to about their information, the angrier they are because their families have kept them in the dark.

I bought the book and read it from cover to cover. I brought it to counseling with me. I continued to reach out to Chuck, who had gone completely silent by this time—probably in a state of panic by the psychologist's report about Ren, asking him if we could please speak about the boys' donor status in counseling.

My psychologist was extremely distressed with the situation and had never counseled any donor conceived children or parents, but was insistent that this was an issue that needed to be dealt with as immediately. By then, my other attorney had decided that he would run for a judge's seat himself, and since I didn't feel he was very attentive and would be even <u>more</u> distracted during a judicial campaign, I sought other counsel.

Chuck did go to one counseling session during that year and yelled at me during the entire visit. He belted out that everything that was wrong with the boys was because of me, stood up and marched around the room, and pointed his finger in my face in front of the counselor -- the same one who had written the report about Ren. He never went back to any of the other scheduled counseling visits, although I tried to get him there. By that time, I was more focused on getting the boys help than I was fearful of Chuck. I was familiar with the finger-pointing outbursts because this was one of Chuck's special talents. He used finger pointing for his board of directors, former bosses, and anybody else he was at war with.

The delay of seeking other counsel and the time allocation for allowing Chuck to follow through with counseling led into the New Year. I'd just retained an attorney of good reputation. What my new counsel told me is that Chuck had retained the new judge's ex-law partner who had even run and raised funds for his campaign in the immediate prior year. In my district, the court systems apparently did not prohibit this obvious bias concern, and placed no restrictions on any relationships between judges and attorneys.

I'd already interviewed one attorney in a neighboring city who had said that not only did this judge refuse to recuse himself from cases his own firm represented, but that no one in court was winning against his law partner. This attorney, a 20-year family court veteran, also said this judge was going to be a horrible judge. How angry I was at myself for not heeding my earlier instincts and listening to my attorney instead!

My new attorney, who worked for the District Attorney prosecuting criminal cases, wasn't intimidated, but made a clear point about being concerned about the judge's bias. But he said since there was a prior judicial order for counseling, there shouldn't be a problem enforcing the counseling order. Legal fees were billed faxing a letter asking Chuck's new attorney to please have his client attend counseling as ordered. There was never any response to the letter, and Chuck never attended another counseling session. We verified receipt of the letter. What I didn't realize then is that Chuck knew already that he wouldn't have to comply with orders ever again.

El Roi Appears

One of the lovely side effects of my court battles with Chuck was that I developed panic attacks. I somehow had the ability to feel my throat closing in when Chuck was even thinking about filing a case-- before it ever hit an attorney's office. It's interesting that this same choking sensation goes all the way back to the incident a few weeks before we were married. Had I known I'd be paying for (my own) failure to escape for over 20 years, I'm sure I would have chosen a different path. I'd have still 'had' Ren and Gray, because they were meant to be exactly who they ended up being. It's interesting to me that God let me make so many mistakes in staying with Chuck, but I would never give birth to Chuck's biological children. I am still not sure what spiritual significance this has.

I called my attorney and told him that I was going through episodes at night of holding my throat and gasping for air, and I knew that Chuck was filing some malicious case. My attorney thought I was crazy, and said, "There is no reason Chuck would be filing, because Chuck is the one who is ignoring court orders." I tried to find comfort in that, but that the twinge in my gut told me Chuck was coming for me.

During that period of weeks, I tried to focus on my business and the kids, as I had no desire to go into any formal battle with Chuck. Since he still refused to complete counseling, and I was in a state of limbo on what to do. It cost thousands to file any case, and based on what I'd heard about the judge, it would only harm us to move forward with any enforcement. Multiple outside attorneys were reporting that nobody was getting anywhere with the judge against his former law partner. Ren wasn't any better or worse, and Chuck had laid off his more obvious outbursts since he'd been exposed by the psychologist's letter.

It was a cold, depressing day, and I'd dropped into a local restaurant to grab a soup and sit for a minute outside my office. To add to the misery, I'd looked up and there was Chuck, reading a contract with his glasses down on his nose. He saw me, but as always, did not speak or acknowledge me. I wondered if anyone ever noticed how he acted when in my presence, with a constant scowl on his face. I also wondered if that stack of papers he held was something he was filing against me. I felt terrorized just to be in the same building as him. I looked down, trying to focus on the soup since I had already been served, and I distractedly checked my email on my phone.

An email dribbled down into my inbox, and I blinked twice and closed my eyes for about 5 seconds, and reopened them, praying that it would still be there. A woman, Sasha Miller, who identified herself as the mother of children from the donor number that I had used, sent a communication introducing herself. She'd found a post I'd made long ago on a donor registry, reaching out for possible half siblings or connections. My heart jumped nearly out of my chest as I hurriedly finished my soup, paid my bill, and left the restaurant, making a beeline to my office. I don't think I looked back at Chuck.

At my office, I reread the email, and answered, "yes, yes, yes, here I am!" or something of that nature, perhaps in the middle of my brain going haywire with sheer delight. Then, it seems like one of us said something like, "Maybe at some point we should share pictures?" We must have been kindred spirits because neither of us waited to get to know each other at all (one of us could have been a serial killer) and the photos of our kids shot through cyberspace. It didn't take DNA testing to immediately see that the kids were related. Later followed baby pictures that convinced me that I could have easily picked up the wrong child at the preschool had we lived in the same town.

Over the next 6-8 weeks, Sasha and I exchanged emails that were full of details about our kids: what they liked to do, their fashion preferences, their personalities, and their sports abilities. What came to light was that our children had been raised very similarly, and Sasha and I had much in common. Our professions were similar, our viewpoints on child rearing, our aspirations for our families, and above all, we each had a strong faith in God.

Sasha's children knew they were donor kids starting when they were little. Her husband Tim was very supportive of being honest (Sasha had suffered miscarriages) and while the children had been told, there had not been a considered need to find siblings until then. Sasha had been inspired by a story that appeared in the news about two sisters who ended up in the same dorm building at college, many states away, and then inadvertently found out they were half-sisters by the same donor. These girls had become best friends, and while on a shopping trip, had purchased the same exact sweater! The sisters had flourished in their lives since finding each other, and their story was truly heartwarming.

When I brought the information about the found siblings to my psychologist, he demanded that the children needed to be told as soon as possible about both their donor conception and the new siblings. I was overjoyed to have the collaboration of a professional, and since the counseling had been ordered by a judge already, I knew I was acting in a completely responsible way.

The counselor also demanded that to preserve Ren and Gray's relationship with Chuck, that he needed to be the one to tell the boys. This would give Chuck control of the information, and further retain the bonds that he had as their father. It had not occurred to me how important this was, but I wanted the "telling" to be done absolutely correctly, as we'd already far breached how long the deception had gone on in their lives, and I knew that I was to blame for this as well.

The counselor also pointed out that it was so much more psychologically appealing to introduce found relatives into the mix, especially teenagers in the same age range as Ren and Gray, with the same interests, than dumping on the boys that they had an anonymous donor that they may never meet. He suggested that I use the photos of the children to introduce the subject, and to lay those all out before beginning to tell Ren and Gray.

I didn't realize it at the time, and the words did not come to me, that El Roi (*The God Who Sees*) had just visited me after years of wandering and desolation. I felt that I could not live my own Truth for fear of protecting Chuck and everyone else in the family who might be uncomfortable with that Truth. What I had been missing in the mix is that Ren and Gray had their own Truth as well, that they deserved to know about.

Sasha's addition to my life made me eternally not alone in this world. I knew that even if something happened to me, Ren and Gray would always have the other children to connect with, as well as at least 2 adults who completely understood who they were. I'd always wanted more children and I already felt that Sasha's kids were partly mine, and mine were partly hers. I felt a sisterhood with her that I can't easily describe but that has sustained me through times of grief which persisted far past the events in this chapter.

I remember being on a plane for work (I have a slight fear of flying) immediately after finding out about the kids and Sasha, before Ren and Gray knew, and thinking, "I could die right now, and I'd be perfectly ok." I hadn't realized how trapped I was in a world that pleased only other people and had ignored my own reality. *The God Who Sees* had seen me, although I was not able to fully realize the full impact of His message yet.

The Telling

I sent Chuck an email about finding the siblings and told him since he wasn't communicating or going to counseling, that email was the only way to communicate with him. I set a date which was at the beginning of a week's holiday from school, and invited Chuck to participate in a family meeting. Gray and Ren were both good students, and I didn't want them to get derailed related to tests and assignments if the news threw them off emotionally.

Chuck did not respond to the email at all, but had his attorney respond to my attorney the day of the meeting, and they demanded "allowing counseling to work" -- remarkably, this was the same counseling that Chuck had refused to go to for months. By then, I was done with all his games and hijinks and knew this was (and my attorney admitted this) just a delay to try to get a court order to stop me from telling the boys. We already knew Chuck's attorney was already known for never losing in the judge's courtroom. He got whatever he asked for, regardless of what it was, or what the history was.

The meeting remained in place, and Chuck brought his wife Monica, and I had Cody there. It was at my home, and the boys were already questioning prior to Chuck getting there as to why there was a family meeting. Everyone came into the family room and sat down. As the counselor suggested, I laid the sibling photos out on a table, and Chuck began to speak. He told the Ren and Gray that he was not their biological father, and I said not a word until he was finished. I thought his speech went pretty well.

Ren looked at the photos and said, "I don't remember taking any of these pictures" which was very amusing to me since the siblings looked so much alike that Ren thought that they were of he and Gray. I proceeded to tell Ren and Gray that the kids in the photos were their half siblings, and that their mom had contacted me, and we'd been talking for several weeks. The first thing that Gray and Ren brought up was wanting to meet the new siblings, to which I replied, "We are trying to arrange that as soon as possible."

Then Gray pushed back in his chair and to my absolute shock declared, "Mom, I've known about this for years." He said, "I knew that I wasn't related to Dad because there was nothing on me that even looked like Dad. Is Ren even my brother?" Then I realized, sadly, that this illusion had gone on way too long; this child was sitting alone wondering all this in the dark!

I told Gray, "Of course you know he is your brother and if you remember, our DNA tests prove that." Then Gray recalled that he'd seen how Ren was his full brother in the results, and the questioning of that issue was over. How sad that Gray had to go through that stressful thought process of wondering if his brother was related to him! Gray admitted that he thought he was adopted, and that Ren was not his brother. How awful to think? I never asked Gray this, but I wonder if he even thought that he'd been the product of some infidelity on my part. This brought to light how truly late we were in bringing the truth to Ren and Gray, and how right the psychologist was that the boys needed to be told immediately.

I watched Chuck become highly agitated when discussions of the DNA tests came up. Since I was used to everything causing him to erupt, this was nothing new to me. Then the boys very happily dispersed, Chuck and Monica left, and we all went to bed. The next day, Ren and Gray went to their weekday visit with Chuck. A counselor I knew had seen them out with him and remarked to me in a text that the boys seemed to be extremely happy. I reported to Chuck in a text that I felt that the boys were doing great, to which he responded with one word: "good".

Not a single bad word happened as a result of the meeting between Ren, Gray, and Chuck, and the boys continued asking me questions about the siblings. Ren asked me if he would ever meet his donor. I told him I wasn't sure.

Ren and Gray still hadn't contacted the siblings, and the siblings had not reached out to Ren and Gray. I think both sides were a little fearful. I took the boys to visit the counselor to talk about their new revelation. Since Gray was the oldest, the counselor suggested that he should be the one to contact the other teenagers first. Within five minutes of leaving the psychologist's office, all of the kids were on social media exchanging messages and photos. I asked the counselor later if he felt Ren and Gray had taken the news well, and he said that they were thrilled, and in great shape mentally.

I felt even more blessed to hear this and to know that we'd "pushed through" the telling without any injury to their relationship with Chuck or with me.

I believe to this day that the happy event of finding out there were actual live half-siblings overshadowed any negatives that would have been associated with finding out they were from an anonymous donor.

It may sound strange that I had to handle this situation this way, but Chuck went months without communicating, and his court antics had already blown a hole in our everyday lives. Things were going so well; I'd managed to avert disaster in telling the boys, and I began to wonder where my choking panic attacks were coming from. I would find out soon enough.

A New Case

Sasha and I had agreed on a visit for introducing the kids, and it involved us flying to where they were, out of state. Since including Chuck was what I was supposed to do on everything, I invited him to come out with us for the meeting. I received no response. I'd given Chuck about 2 weeks' notice and contacted him as soon as the visit was arranged.

Not surprisingly, Chuck went silent again as he usually did when he was displeased. The day before we were to take off, the attorney emails started flying, starting that fun spinning wheel that creates inflated billings that many of you know about by now. The first was a threatening letter from Chuck's attorney to mine about my "immorality" in my telling Ren and Gray the truth about their conception. It's funny that the whole case was based on me telling the boys, when it was actually Chuck who told them that he wasn't their biological father. I merely introduced the sibling part after the telling. The "immorality" letter was signed by his attorney, who was a politician in my state and who had actually just voted against rights associated with assisted reproductive technologies (ART) that very year.

Cody, my husband, had already suggested that the boys and I needed to stay over in another town in a hotel before leaving the next morning, since the communication had become hostile. During that stress-filled evening, Sasha (the siblings' mom and my new friend) text me that they had prayed for a good meeting for the children during their Bible study. That little text kept me from having a complete nervous breakdown that night, and I will always remember it as a sign that we were all headed in the right direction.

The next morning, Ren and Gray and I arrived at the airport. Ren and I headed to the breakfast café to grab something to eat before boarding. When we looked across the room, we could not believe our eyes. There was Monica (Chuck's wife) in the airport restaurant! Ren looked right into her face, and she turned away, not speaking.

Suddenly, my attorney started texting me not to respond to any texts or emails, because Chuck was trying to get an order from the judge to stop us from leaving. I was a complete wreck until the wheels were up on our second flight. I felt as if I was in a conspiracy movie in which bad guys were chasing me and popping up everywhere. On the last leg of the flight, I calmed down once the plane took off since I knew Chuck did not have the resources to hire fighter jets!

The sibling meetup weekend went wonderfully; the kids all had an immediate bond, and Sasha and I thoroughly enjoyed our visit. Her husband Tim made a campfire, and all the teenagers did the entire weekend was hang out and play sports. Gray received a call while there from Chuck in which Chuck told Gray that he had been left out of the trip, not been invited, and that he'd wanted to come, but didn't know about it. This audacious lying to the children continued to be a theme in my post-divorce world with Chuck. I always had to keep an email archive of everything I sent Chuck.

While on our sibling visit, on Sunday, we'd gone with the kids and their parents to a contemporary evangelical church. I cried during one of the songs at the absolute grace of having been able to sew up

Ren and Gray's Truth, and enrich their lives. Truly this last few months had been a spiritual awakening.

I even found out through Sasha that she had developed an illness after giving birth that prevented her from having any more children. It turns out she was the one who released the vials right before I called the clinic, back when I was sure that Gray would never have a sibling. Out of the millions of people on the planet, who would have thought that Sasha and I would meet years later?

The kids now control their own relationships. Sasha and I continue to be close friends. We have a special bond. Chuck continued his campaign of destruction. I received a call from my attorney that he'd received a filing copy from Chuck's attorney. I had a weekend planned with Ren and Gray and I didn't want it spoiled by another one of Chuck's phony cases, so I told my attorney to hold onto it for a few days. That was one of the smartest decisions I've ever made, to enjoy a small oasis of peace before the next storm.

Finally, I did get the case filing. In it, Chuck claimed that I was immoral and likely damaging the boys by allowing them to meet their siblings and know about their genetics. Chuck also claimed that I had denied him access to the boys when he wanted them, or when they wanted to see him. He claimed that I did not communicate medical information about the boys.

Chuck filed for a change in custody due to a change in circumstances, detailing his need to bond with the boys, and again stating that I was immoral and that he should be the domiciliary parent, which is a term in my state used for decision-making capacity on schools, medical, and sports activities.

During the weeks leading up to the case filing, Gray had developed a cyst in his cheek area near his jaw. I'd taken him to the pediatrician and notified Chuck I was doing this. Then the pediatrician had referred us to a specialist. I kept emailing Chuck about the issue, and he'd kept ignoring me. I'd even phoned Chuck and asked why he hadn't responded, and he seemed so uncomfortable on the phone, that I knew something was up then. He was avoiding having medical discussions so that he could prove his case.

Ren had a rash several months earlier, and I'd taken him to the pediatrician and paid upwards of $100 for treatment cream, plus the visit cost. I'd reported Ren's issue to Chuck, who suggested a dermatology contact in the city he worked in. I'd politely declined acting on that at the time, because he'd just been to the doctor, and I didn't want to pay twice for treatment. In Chuck's filing, he'd claimed I'd blatantly refused his input on Ren's medical care by refusing to go to this second physician, which made no sense, because Ren was already being treated.

Anytime Chuck was up to his antics, he'd either send flowery, wordy emails flourished with details to prove he was involved on any subject he was about to use in court, or stoic silence on anything he knew he wasn't abiding by. These were the markers in the road which oddly **followed** my panic attacks, which were always prophetic.

The case wording was so ridiculous and so provably wrong, that my attorney copied the 4-inch-thick batch of discovery papers and hand delivered it to Chuck's attorney's office. Included in the discovery: the clinical psychologist's report about Chuck emotionally abusing Ren and the recommendation that all Chuck's visitation be stopped until Chuck got into counseling, all of the emails about medical issues that I'd contacted Chuck about (at least 15 of them), the proof of email notification about the trip with the siblings, and a copy of the letter faxed to Chuck's attorney asking him to go to counseling as ordered.

Chuck's attorney ignored all the discovery and refused to meet with us. I couldn't believe I'd gone in 5 short months from getting a report that Chuck shouldn't even have visitation with Ren, to getting charged with being immoral and losing control of the boys and humiliated with lies before a court. What was worse, Chuck was making a public issue out of the boys' genetics during a time in which they needed to feel confident, accepted, and peaceful. Poor Cody was out thousands of dollars—if it had not been for him, I'd have had to just fold and let Chuck win every time, because I could never have afforded legal fees like that.

Since custody was in play and the boys were teenagers, my attorney wanted to privately interview them to see what they truly wanted. This was so that their wishes would be followed. Did they want to spend more time with Chuck? If so, then that needed to be addressed. In meeting with them, the attorney told them they may have to negotiate and agree to give Chuck an extra night every other week, just to satisfy him (my attorney knew that the judge might be biased and didn't want to take any chances with our outcome). The boys decided that Chuck could have the Sunday evening every other week that he complained about, giving him 3 evenings with Ren and Gray on his weekends. This only extended their time with Chuck to the next morning when they were to be dropped off at school.

My attorney told the boys that the judge had already agreed openly in a status meeting to give the boys what they wanted in custody. The real concern to me was that the entire case was full of falsehoods, and that it seemed to be just a mechanism to get before the judge. My attorney had faith in his own skills and what he perceived as a relationship with the judge, and also thought the word of the judge on this topic could be trusted.

The day of the trial, the boys went in to talk to the judge, and my attorney told me that Chuck's attorney tried to twist Gray's words to get him to agree to more time, but that in the end Gray had said what the boys agreed upon in my attorney's office. Ren had let his brother talk on his behalf, since he was younger. I felt that I was serving my children up for slaughter, and it turned out that I was.

Chuck lied on the stand at least 8 times, with the discovery presented in court, with copies of emails, notifications, and the proof that Chuck was in direct disregard for the counseling order that the prior judge had been set to hear just 4 months earlier, before this new judge was even sworn in. Also presented in court was the proof of notification sent to Chuck's attorney notifying that Chuck was in violation of the counseling order. The two court-ordered counselors testified on my behalf as to the relationship between Chuck and Ren, acknowledging the screaming at Ren, and communication issues with Chuck.

The judge refused to enforce the counseling order and did not even make Chuck pay his share of the counseling that he was ordered to do. I was already out thousands. The judge even made a biting comment to me that if I 'liked' the clinical psychologist, that I could keep going. He completely disregarded the fact that I had been ordered by the prior judge to go to this specific psychologist, and that I was following court orders. He gave Chuck more custody of Ren and Gray. He refused to declare me the domiciliary parent, even with Chuck lying on the stand, the case being completely falsified, and the judge's words in court negating the entire filing, admitting that no damage had been done to Ren and Gray. Even Chuck admitted to the judge on the stand that nothing negative had happened with the boys due to the disclosure about their genetics.

When I arrived home from court, both boys were crying. Ren collapsed in the laundry room. Chuck showed up to get them and take them away. I could barely stand up. Cody managed to calm everyone down. But I had been paraded in front of a firing squad for something I didn't do, my private life exposed to strangers. That same day, Gray found the photo of the judge on Chuck's attorney's website in an advertising banner photo, on the front page. We snapped a screenshot of the web page.

When Gray confronted Chuck about the website, Chuck told him another lie about when the judge was elected. I felt as if I'd failed Ren; failed both of them, and that Ren would now be further at risk. Chuck was rewarded handsomely for his lies and for ignoring court orders for months and months. After hearing what happened, Gray declared out loud, "The judge lied to us."

The next weeks that followed were the worst weeks I remember in my life. A runner for 5 years, I could barely get around the block. I cried uncontrollably. I sat alone, without Cody for the most part, since he'd had to go back to the ranch. I'd never been without Ren and Gray for that long since they were born. I'd always been their primary caregiver. My faith in right and wrong was gone.

Despite what I'd been through with Chuck, I had refused to say too much of it in court, even though his attorney prodded me in that direction, presumably for the domiciliary parent trophy. As you should know, as a woman, no matter if you were half-beaten to death by an ex, if you dare say anything negative about your ex in family court, that is a slam dunk against you having custody or control of your kids.

I knew deep down that God had stepped in, allowing Sasha and the boys into our lives at a critical point in Ren and Gray's development. But I was having trouble with the equity of the situation, not to mention the trauma of knowing that Ren was in a dangerous place with Chuck emotionally. I'd already been through so much. Would it ever end?

If Gray and Ren ever wanted to do anything with Chuck that was outside our custody schedule in the past, which was quite rare, I'd readily agreed to it, because it was the right thing to do. I knew that I'd never have that same courtesy from Chuck. His time with them was a commodity he possessed. He was going to get his pound of flesh.

Time marched on, and after a while, my depression eased. But Chuck was now free to do anything he wanted because he now knew nothing would ever be enforced in this courtroom. I wish court officials understood that when you reward a narcissist for lying in court, they are emboldened to abuse you further, knowing that they will never be held accountable. This goes for court systems that do not enforce orders when the victim has brought fees to get the issue heard. The message it sends is loud and clear. If they only knew what these poor victims go through after trial! Sometimes we are better off just letting the perpetrator get away with it because we as victims are both set back financially and will be further harassed.

After this, I began to get calls about Ren's emotional state from his school, and even under the threat of being filed on again, I got Ren back into counseling to deal with Chuck. There were many times I feared getting caught taking Ren to counseling secretly, and what that penalty would be if Chuck decided to file a case? Loss of my rights as a parent? Full custody for Chuck? Jail time for me, just because the judge decided that? Who knew? All I knew is that Ren needed counseling, and I wouldn't be around to protect him forever, and Chuck had more access to Ren now since the judge had rewarded Chuck's lies.

I found out later that my attorney (I'd expressed concerns about getting the boys' wishes in writing before trial) did not demand what is called a Westermeyer Hearing, in which all conversations from children are recorded in judge's chambers. He trusted that the judge would not be so biased as to lie about his intentions in the case.

After my experience, I'd tell parents who are faced with a similar situation to always demand a Westermeyer hearing because that way a transcript of what a child actually says is readily available, and it might prevent what happened to us. I'd already sat down with Gray when he was 16 (when I went through the attorney bullying) and explained that he was plenty old enough to decide where he wanted to live; I'd already made that clear to both boys. The boys wanted to talk to the judge. They were fighting Chuck's legal action and their valiance was slammed to the ground. The children coming into an unrecorded judge's chambers was a setup by the unscrupulous politician attorney.

Even after this horrific experience, I would learn that I still was still driving that car that Chuck didn't like the color of.

Filing Complaints

Only if you are a real bonehead do you do what I did after this. I was still so incensed about Gray finding the judge's photo on the attorney's webpage the day of court, that I filed an ethics complaint with my state. Little did I know, the ethics board that was in my region basically works to protect attorneys, and this attorney was a legislator. To the best of my knowledge, all he got was a phone call and was able to remove the photo from his website. All I got was the "middle finger" by the system.

I went to the trouble of pointing out the blatant ethics violation, only to be ignored and subsequently put in danger of retaliation later when Chuck decided to come after me again. This is how I know that in many districts, the system doesn't mean anything as it relates to accountability—it is all just a game to control the dialogue.

I filed a judicial complaint as well. What they tell you in my state is that you cannot discuss the complaint with anyone, but the judicial commission in my state can operate in secrecy with no checks and balances. The commission never contacted any of the witnesses that I listed. They allowed the judge to go answer the complaint in private, with (this is stated in writing by the commission) no recorded transcript. All the judge had to do was give his version of what was said by Gray and Ren in the closed session (which was also unrecorded) and his word **only** was used. I was not allowed to attend, my attorney who is now a judge was never contacted, and my children were not allowed to give their side. The system is set up only to protect judges.

After this, I was going to be royally screwed to go in front of this judge when Chuck pulled his antics again. It wouldn't matter what I did or didn't do, Chuck would win anyway, and I would be punished. But at that point, I didn't think there was anything else for Chuck to come after me about.

If your children are young, and you end up in this type situation, think hard and research thoroughly the quality of the ethics in your state. If it's too risky for your children and you, do not report ethical violations. The system may not protect you, and then you and your kids will suffer if dragged back into that courtroom. If I had an ethical judicial system, I'd have been able to:

- Successfully achieve a recusal merely by stating the obvious -- that Chuck's attorney was a law partner of the judge and had actually run the judge's election campaign.

- Gain recognition and the enforcement of penalties for the attorney and judge brandishing their picture together for advertising purposes on the attorney's website (this was an overt violation of a Judicial Canon) on the day of my court case.

- The children meeting with the judge would have been recorded.

- The discovery alone that I provided, and the lying that Chuck did in court should have stopped my case in its tracks and sent Chuck packing, possibly with him paying my court and attorney fees.

As it stood for me, Ren and Gray were teenagers by the time our case was over, and based on what I was hearing in the legal environment as it related to my district, there was not going to be any enforcement of ethics or accountability thrust upon this attorney or the judge. I had nothing to lose anymore.

In the end, I know I did the right thing by adding to the judicial complaints about this particular judge, but unfortunately, no one was corroborating the number of appeals filed with the number of judicial complaints. No one was looking into campaign contributions in relation to court 'winners' either.

The slow, creaky, unscrupulous system allows too many biased decisions if you are unlucky enough to be on the other side of the tracks with your legal defense. In my area, some attorneys in adjoining districts simply refused to try cases against the legislator partner attorney because they faced certain loss.

The parties that did end up in unmovable cases would often settle for whatever the other side wanted in order to avoid worse outcomes in front of the judge.

Shouldn't all children be provided unbiased court officers and judges, and shouldn't all parents be afforded the peace of knowing that they will be treated fairly? Should a parent know in advance when they have spent thousands of dollars protecting their children, that they will lose only because of what judge they face?

At that point, I thought I was done with Chuck in court (wrong again).

The Retreat

I had the opportunity to participate as a chaperone at a church youth encampment retreat in the mountains that invited inspirational speakers from all over. It was a beautiful place to be, located in green rolling mountains. For most of the conference, I was at the group's home base helping cook meals and wash loads of shorts, underwear, and socks. I'd chosen to be more of a "room mom" than a counselor for that retreat.

That day, however, we were caught up and I'd decided to go to one of the events. The speaker began talking about the feeling of being outcast with the very large group of mostly smiling youth. Then, the mood began to change, and the emotions of the kids started surfacing. The number of kids at this Christian retreat who felt alienated were teeming. When the minister began speaking about Hagar, which means in ancient Hebrew "The Stranger", my own spiritual light came on.

As she continued speaking, I realized that the marginalization of Hagar in the story related so closely to my marginalization in my marriage to Chuck as more of a child bearer than a wife. I'd heard the story, but in my upbringing, the subject of Hagar was almost avoided, perhaps because no one knew what to do with her from a moral standpoint.

What was also omitted was the discussion of how Hagar's station in life as a maidservant would entail whatever her mistress wanted her to do. There were no sexual harassment laws or "Me Too" movements. Hagar was just doing her job when she slept with

Abraham to produce his offspring. Granted, my situation was far more overt due to the donor circumstances, but through history women have been repeatedly capitalized on as means to an end. There wasn't more of an arms-length distance between Hagar's role and mine. The method of getting there was just a test tube away.

The fact that I'd been victimized after escaping my marriage to Chuck added to my isolation. My children and I had wandered through a desert wasteland of court cases and lies, and we had been unable to tell our own story. I realized during that conference that if I had never left Chuck, Ren and Gray likely would have not known of their genetics until many years later.

Having been in a more traditional setting, I had also felt squelched from sharing my concerns or discussing Ren and Gray's conception with my friends. I had even felt unable to discuss Chuck's physical abuse early on, and also his glaring emotional abuse. By saying "unable" it sounds as if there were chains holding me from disclosure, but it was more about pleasing the people around me socially and not being viewed as a failure, because I believed that the failure would be mine, not Chuck's. Many girls are brought up in an environment in which "making waves" is not Christian behavior, and we are often blamed for our failed marriages.

Events that happened in my childhood were strongly influential in my suppression of the nature of my marriage to Chuck. I had learned to be a "pleaser" because when I was only being myself there were often negative results. There will be a book for later about WHY some of us end up with abusive mates (*Before El Roi*). Hint: it isn't always your fault.

The speaker went on to tie together the station of being an outcast with the journey of Hagar, and how she cried out in the wilderness to God as she stepped away from her dying son Ishmael. An oasis appeared in the desert, saving Ishmael. Hagar was the first to ever declare God as El Roi, (pronounced el-ho-hee) which means *The God Who Sees Me*. I felt that my story perfectly paralleled Hagar's story, and that God reached through time and space and brought Sasha and her children, Ren and Gray's siblings, into view.

The darkness I'd walked through with Chuck seemed never-ending, and our station being subject to his attacks had left me feeling hopeless and invisible, as if we would never be seen.

To this day, while writing this book, I am still living in a somewhat murky place where few know my story. I believe that my story is brought to you for a specific purpose; to let you know that God Sees You as He saw me, even though my journey is decades long and still continues; with stumbling, doubts, and many tears.

Hagar's story, in my special mission and illumination, speaks to the evils that oppression creates, and the redemption that can happen when you reach out and ask El Roi, *The God Who Sees*, to intervene.

Mean Church

My church was suffering from member losses and specifically losses of young families, and I was pretty sure why. Years ago a friend of mine and I had petitioned the senior operating board of our church to add some special nursery activities and a Mother's Morning Out program which we volunteered to manage, and we were turned down by the board with the reason that the decision "was too fast". Over 15 years later, the church still had not done what was needed or put the personnel in place to retain or grow members with small children. The church had funded hard asset acquisitions, additional land, building renovations, and tithe drives, but it had been lagging in the changing landscape of churchgoing families.

For the youth group to go to the annual mountain retreat required a fundraise that the parents had to do each year to replenish the cash needed to cover the camp fees per youth, rent a house, and pay expenses. There was no issue with this per se except that it tended to place the weightiest burden on the people who had the least time or money to begin with. I remember as a participating parent for years, the bone numbing fatigue from the fundraisers and the mere $50 I was able to put in either as a donation or in "buying" something, then having barely enough funds to pay the fee for the camp. The wealthier members dumped thousands into the fundraise, which made it work. But some of us were struggling day-to-day and could barely participate financially. Each time I participated it yielded a financial and time hole that I had to fill in some other way.

I'd spontaneously funded the pizza for our group during that last fundraising event, since the people helping were going to pass out from hunger if I didn't, and because no one on the church staff had arranged food for the people and youth participating. No one showed up with fishes and loaves, either. I'd had to submit that receipt for pizzas to the bookkeeper. I then received a long-winded lashing that left me feeling embarrassed for even asking for reimbursement, and I was angry that faithful folks who had donated all their time for that entire week were being criticized for needing a morsel to eat that night. Then Chuck decided that he wouldn't reimburse me for his half of the additional fee I'd had to pay for Ren's camp slot.

There was a deadline on paying the fee and I'd paid it. I'd reminded Chuck twice by email of the deadline, and he had ignored each reminder. I'd phoned the church to ask for a receipt for the payment, and I was told brusquely "we don't give out receipts" by the same worker who had required the receipt for the pizza.

I'd had to get the minister involved to force the bookkeeper to issue a receipt to me. Chuck still refused to pay me. He knew there would be no enforcement in court for this expense.

Then came the absolute blow to me that I never recovered from in my church. I had just dropped off another donation at the church that I'd barely been able to do for a Christmas charity program. I served on the youth advisory council, and I was a regular donator of time and money when there was a need.

There was a youth party at my house that weekend for a holiday celebration. I'd been running around like a crazy person trying to get my house ready for that party, and I barely had enough funds to make it through the month.

That was when Chuck phoned me and informed me on a Thursday afternoon that the church had called him and invited him to be in a ceremony in the main service that Sunday, 3 days away, to light the Advent candle with the Ren and Gray, and would I like to participate with Cody? I'd just been to the church office, just spoken to the minister, and there was no mention of any invitation to participate. Yet I had been left out as Ren and Gray's mother in this regular traditional family segment in a church I'd been a member in for over 20 years. Cody was at the ranch, and there was no way I could get him over to participate that quickly.

After Chuck had dragged me to court on lie after lie and cost my family thousands very recently, and cost Ren and Gray peace in their lives, standing in the front of my church lighting a candle with Chuck wasn't in my wheelhouse anyway.

I can't begin to explain how alienating this was for me. I'd found out through the minister that the church secretary had been in charge of the selection. I'd just talked to her, and she made no mention of the advent candle that weekend. But when I told the minister about my experience, he apologized but made no effort to move the event to a weekend when I could have participated. He made no effort towards correcting that I was left out of my own children's event. Even if I hadn't been a member for over 20 years, it would have been unconscionable for any church management to leave out a parent from such an invitation. I certainly, even in the face of what actions Chuck had taken against me, wouldn't have left him out of the equation had the situation been reversed, and I would have declined the invitation if all parties could not have participated. To do otherwise would have been classless.

Now, I was never one to embrace public events anyway and I generally avoid pomp and circumstance. It was more about being hurt by my church than about not being in the religious "show". I chose to sit the Advent Candle ceremony out and stayed at home, while Chuck was honored along with the boys and Monica during the service. I did not have the energy to fight anymore.

I did continue to go to church when I could and did participate in another fundraiser for the benefit of the children. But I could not ever feel the same about my church nor could I view it as a support system.

When I had tried to disclose what was going on with Ren to my minister, I'd left feeling embarrassed, dismissed, and patronized. I also felt that I was not believed. My church definitely wanted my fundraising efforts, donations, and time, but it did not want me. So, I slid quietly away. I did not leave my church, but I know that my church left me.

After my experience, my church lost 15 families through one form of alienation or another. My place of faith had gone tone-deaf to personal relationships and caregiving. It had become a field of discouragement and conflict. Sasha, the siblings' mom, said perhaps the wisest thing: "Sometimes the devil just gets in your church."

I'll just leave this thought there. I don't think I could do any better than Sasha in summarizing the situation. Sometimes the Holy Spirit just gets muddled in your church, especially when it either becomes a social outlet or in some of the worst and most embarrassing cases, a political platform for the aspirations of its leaders. If there are personality-related forces, herding behaviors, and phony objectives at play, your church will have conflict. If those things become dominant, your fellowship can become blind spiritually. When that happens, it is like turning around a giant cruise ship to correct course.

Continued Antics

One of the earmarks of Chuck's methodology was to do the opposite of whatever we agreed upon for the sole purpose of creating chaos. This included agreements on claiming children on tax returns. If we agreed that I would claim Ren, he claimed Ren. If we agreed that I would claim Gray, he'd claim Gray. It was all part of Chuck's special gift.

Because I made far less money, and Gray was certainly at my home more than Chuck's, we'd agreed that I would file the federal financial aid paperwork for Gray, who was graduating at the top of his class. Chuck then backdoored me and claimed Gray on his taxes. This could potentially have damaged Gray's financial aid if verification documents were required. I'd already found my forged signature on a return I had never seen with income I never knew about in years past when I was married to Chuck.

Chuck had already lost his driver's and hunting licenses over not filing state taxes. "Chuck running amok" was no pretty picture, and I was trying my hardest to get Gray the scholarships he deserved, and a fair shot at some of the schools he wanted to apply to. Chuck would give one face to Gray in assurances and a completely different story to me.

Chuck soon went after control of Gray's college choice. Gray had been offered a full scholarship to a top-ranked engineering school. It happened to be Cody's alma mater. Another top ranked school, exactly as far away, offered no scholarships and would have put Gray tens of thousands of dollars per year in debt. Which college did

Chuck recommend to Gray? You got it. As stunning as this was, Chuck would rather Gray be in six figure debt than to go to Cody's alma mater, even though the college offering the full scholarship was in the top 10 rankings in what Gray was majoring in.

Gray did make the right choice and opted wisely to forego having college debt. When your kids are finally old enough to make their own decisions, you as a "victim parent" of child manipulation will cheer to the heavens, because finally your life isn't dictated by a crazy person. Your children will have the opportunity to find their own pathways.

Destructive Women

After going through an overt miscarriage of justice and corruption in our case once, I was bound and determined never to appear before the judge again. I was fearful of Chuck starting another round of litigation, since the psychologist who saw him once told me that Chuck thrived on anger and trying to destroy me or discredit me using the court system.

Chuck was waiting for his next move. This time, it had to do with Gray being almost 18. Chuck's multiple contempt violations had led to my previous attorney establishing an en globo, or flat rate support. It had mostly covered the very expensive insurance and school tuition. Things had changed, however. Gray was out of high school, but he had enjoyed an almost complete scholarship during his entire high school career. Then Ren entered high school, and Ren's tuition was almost $10,000 (Chuck wouldn't HEAR of public school -- that would have been another court case to fight) including sports and other fees. Health insurance had skyrocketed, but in the family court system, a payee is only allotted a share of the child's component of health insurance. Nothing would be assessed or paid for anything related to Gray since he was now 18, yet Cody and I continued to pay Gray's health insurance and some of his extraneous expenses.

The health insurance component as it relates to child support is a severely outdated calculation. The parent who is required to carry insurance may not even be able to afford their own coverage. Premiums may have doubled or tripled, while the child coverage might only be a few hundred dollars more. Even to a custodial parent with far less income, the support payment could be less than $100 monthly for insurance per child.

Even though our circumstances and expenses had changed to the extent that Chuck should have been paying <u>more</u> than his previously ordered en globo support, I didn't dare try to change it or discuss it. Not only would it cost more to change than I could ever hope to collect, but data in the court system indicated that the judge would only rule in favor of his former law partner.

Therefore, I sat tight and just hoped and prayed that I could make it through the next few years. Chuck began sending me emails several months before Gray's 18th birthday, saying that his attorney told him that he could simply half his child support arbitrarily. I corrected Chuck, reminding him that his support payment included school tuition and insurance and was in force until Ren turned 18.

When Chuck realized that what I told him was true, he began making up amounts that he would propose to pay and to negotiate getting "credit for" tuition at the school, backpedaling on his next two monthly support payments. He had no clue that the high school required ALL of the tuition up front months prior to the beginning of the school year. Chuck's bait and switch emails were happening again; he was trying to trip up the conversation and gain an agreement on support without ever sharing his financial information. But Cody and I weren't about to try to fight Chuck in court. We were going to let Chuck propose something within state guidelines just to avoid another court case.

The fact that Chuck believed that he would always get whatever he wanted meant that I could do nothing but deal with him as if he was an out of control toddler, and try to speak with my attorney to see if we could expect any enforcement of child support at all from the judge.

Meanwhile, Ren was starting to have difficulty again with Chuck's bullying. One morning I got a confidential phone call from the high school counselor, indicating that Ren had spent part of the morning in his office. The counselor told me that Ren was having trouble dealing with Chuck's anger. It was the same old story I'd heard for years since Ren was young. The counselor said that I needed to seek counseling for Ren as soon as possible. I took it upon myself to seek and pay for this since I could expect nothing but obstruction from Chuck and no support from the judge, who hadn't even enforced the prior order for counseling. The re-eruption of this issue made me sit back in my chair and feel defeated and depressed. I had no ethical family court enforcement, and an issue that had emerged again and again since Ren was 10 years old.

A few days after this, I'd confided in a woman that I had been friends with a long time about what I was going through with Ren. This entire disclosure was merely a private conversation due to my genuine concern for Ren. The next thing I knew, this woman, an attorney, had phoned Chuck's attorney to disclose to him what was going on with Ren. I received a call from her, saying to me, "Jess, I have jumped into your business." When she told me what she did, all I could think is, "What kind of friend _ARE_ you?" The last thing I needed was Ren's private information dumped on Chuck's attorney. Chuck's attorney had refused to even look at the discovery my prior attorney had provided them before, and in spite of Chuck lying in court multiple times, had refused to drop Chuck as a client or admit that Chuck's case was completely falsified.

I was mortified. Now, my private information had been disclosed. This woman viewed herself as a political force in our community. She was already using this attorney's corruption in her own family. Cody and I had used her firm's services to defend ourselves against Chuck's actions, and we'd paid thousands of dollars for both confidentiality and representation. She was also a partner in this firm. Attorneys are bound by confidentiality; I would have never imagined that my own disclosure as a friend would end up being vomited to Chuck's attorney without her even asking me.
This was in the context of her deciding to "help".

This busybody twit of a woman began to tell me how she'd made a deal with the attorney to support him for the district attorney's race, which is what he'd demanded as "pay back" for flipping over Chuck and working for me instead. Then, I began to be told what attorneys to see, what to say, and what to do. Why would she do this? I still cannot believe that in the face of my disclosing things honestly to her on a personal level that she decided on the path she took. I believe it was partly her own arrogance about her own "political pull" and her own sense of power in manipulating outcomes.

What she did hurt my chances of ever being able to escape that courtroom without injury again. Be careful who you disclose anything about your children or your court case to. You may end up with a situation that defies anything you ever expected.

Keep it to your very closest "graveyard" friends and your (trusted) attorney. There is corruption everywhere.

Meanwhile, Jessica, the attorney, told me that Mr. Fred would not represent Chuck any further. Chuck, operating on his own agenda, was doing his usual shyster things. I even received an email from him announcing that he would start paying his "new child support" on a certain date, without ever having a judgment, negotiation, or hearing. I informed Chuck that I had not been able to select or meet with an attorney at that point.

It was then that I received a document by email with a signature demand from Mr. Fred's law firm. The paper was one page and did not address percentages of shared expenses, insurance, or tuition at all. To sign it would mean that Chuck would get away with paying less than half what he was paying before, with no legal responsibility for tuition or insurance. The paper was completely blank on most of the issues that I'd chronically had with Chuck related to court ordered support and shared expenses.

I politely emailed Mr. Fred's law clerk, who'd sunnily offered for Chuck and me to just "come by and sign" the document, that I had not had time to meet with my attorney, but that I would try to meet Chuck's deadline. Much to my shock, Chuck soon shorted his support payment by $1400 a month, which put him in contempt of court for the third time.

Cody and I met with the attorney I'd chosen (no one was going to tell me what attorney to hire, not even Mr. Fred) and asked if there was any reason to think that child support would be enforced at all in our district. She said yes; judges can't just ignore support as it is a strict mandate with not much wiggle room. I then contacted my fly by night "friend" Jessica and told her to please make some time to meet with me, as I needed to retain an attorney who understood my case. I informed her that I had a judicial complaint with the judge and that I needed to have dinner with her or a meeting to truly explain to her my situation. I'd told her outright that I needed to retain a certain attorney for my case who had been successful at staving off the judge's crazy rulings, but I also told her how critical my personal situation was.

She couldn't be bothered with this, nodding her head but never taking me up on my request to have dinner or discuss further, and continued, I suppose, to make her deal with Mr. Fred. I cautioned her by email not to do this, as Mr. Fred would stop at nothing to win cases, and if ever achieving the office of District Attorney, people who were innocent would go to prison. She continued to assure me that Mr. Fred would not represent Chuck in any case.

Then it happened: I was served by a deputy at my house. There it was in black and white: Mr. Fred, Chuck's double agent attorney, had signed the filing himself.

Because of the situation, my attorney and I decided to file for a judge recusal, and this would slow down the freight train of Chuck coming after me. I'd hadn't been paid by my company for almost 5 years. I had been looking for employment for a year and a half. I was invisible to the job market as a past-50 female who had only worked for herself for 30 years. I'd written every client I ever had for projects; I'd offered to do writing on a freelance basis; I'd applied for every administrative and low-level clerical job there was.

I was also dealing with Ren's counseling, which was getting increasingly hard to pay for. I'd survived Christmas, but only because of Cody. Cody's family had sold a property in another state we'd eventually hoped to relocate to, and Cody had converted that investment into a small home there. That was a bright spot in my mind and a place to escape on occasion, and we'd vacationed there. One day, we'd consider living there, far away from my state's corruption and economic misery.

Since Mr. Fred was legislator, he could delay cases as long as he was currently in session. This made it convenient for him to not have to deal with cases that he didn't want to. For me, the delay meant starving me out for months and months while Chuck was paying less than 1/3 of the support he'd paid before. Gray had received a full scholarship for college on his own merits. Ren's tuition had continued to go up, as had health insurance. I'd sold my home because it was too expensive. I was in a rent home and was having trouble meeting expenses, especially after Chuck decided that he would pay his "new" support.

I'd saved pages and pages of emails and texts from my so-called "friend" Jessica since by now, I knew everyone around me was subject to corruption. I smelled a rat, and nothing she said about what was going on with Mr. Fred had ever proven true.

Then came the day of the recusal hearing. Before I could even leave the courtroom, my recusal case had been assigned to the only other judge that never ruled against Mr. Fred, since he had been her law clerk long ago.

My courthouse didn't even follow state law in randomly assigning recusal cases; my attorney told me what really happens is that the law clerk meets with the judge that the recusal is being sought from and the judge gets to select what judge hears it. Then, they would make their "arrangements" before the hearings.

Then, Jessica pulled her final and fatal move: she told someone else that I did not authorize her to speak to that I was making a "big mistake" in my attorney selection, and that she needed to intervene by "taking me to dinner" (this is after I'd asked her specifically to spend time with me to hear the details about my case). Here she'd disclosed my private information to Chuck's attorney, and now she was involving another of my associates.

I called my attorney and told her what happened. She phoned this out-of-control twit and asked her what her role was in my case. Quickly Jessica phoned me to complain about how much risk she took on my behalf. I won't go into what I told her, but I pulled no punches in telling her how betrayed I felt, and how dare she put Ren at risk the way that she did! I've not spoken to her since.

Jessica continues to be featured in local/regional articles as a popular and competent female attorney. I think she is a narcissist herself and very dangerous. Her involvement in corruption has put other children at risk because she helps "feed the monster" in the family court system.

The moral of this story is to never trust <u>anybody</u> with personal information, especially if it involves your children, unless it is a proven close friend or your own attorney. Even family members who cannot be trusted with privacy are off limits. This exposure that was caused by this horrible experience cost us thousands of dollars dodging around in the already deep field of manure.

Corruption in The Swamp

After this, I knew that I had to fight. I had to fight with everything I had because I had no other option. If I went before the judge, he could throw me in jail, he could take custody of Ren completely away, he could punish me with penalties -- even though Chuck had abruptly stopped paying his ordered child support. It would cost thousands, and I would lose. Chuck had ignored the order for counseling, and the judge had not only not enforced the counseling, he'd made fun of me in court. I was screwed, no matter what I did.

About that time, it became evident that I was not going to be finding a job. Chuck was never going to have to pay the right support, and I was going under financially. Cody had supported us from a distance for over 8 years and spent thousands protecting the boys and me. Ren recently had engaged in a physical altercation with Chuck that ended with Chuck apologizing to his family, many of them witnessing the event.

When Ren got taller than Chuck, Chuck began to shirk more from his bullying. Ren was now driving and growing up fast. If Chuck got out of line, he could just drive away. I proposed to the boys I'd be thinking about moving to where Cody's other home was to both alleviate expenses and afford us a chance to start over. I told Ren he wouldn't have to go, but that it would be great if he would consider it, as there were excellent schools and state tuition waivers if I were a resident. Gray was already in a distant college, and Ren also wanted out of state options for college.

Ren agreed to consider the move, and I assured him that he'd be able to travel back and forth. I explained to him that I'd tried for years to gain any income, job, or project that would pay. I'd sold my home at an almost $50k loss and I couldn't hang on much longer.

Ren and Gray thought the move was a good idea for me, and Ren seemed positive about considering going along. I had, by that time, put my entire life in God's hands because I couldn't imagine what else I could possibly do to avert the next wave that might hit me from any angle. This whole situation was getting so hard to believe that I felt like I was in a daze. So, with Ren's approval to proceed, my attorney sent a relocation letter to add to the filings before the court. But we still had the recusal hearing ahead of us, and Mr. Fred was using his legislative privilege to delay it, over and over.

Being the analytical type, I decided to do a data set related to the court records on the judge's decisions for later use. I was already envisioning this book. I was incensed that no one could do anything to expose such collusion in court. I made a few phone calls and found out that I could get copies of cases and outcomes by attorney name and firm, filtering them by judge presiding. I managed to get copies of every case that Mr. Fred's firm tried in front of his ex-law partner judge since he'd been elected, as well as copies of other cases by other attorneys NOT associated with Mr. Fred's firm, as a comparison.

After analyzing many dozens of cases, I found that Mr. Fred won ALL of the cases he presented in front of his judge law partner that were filed by his firm. There was only one case, in which the plaintiff was another firm, that showed a favorable outcome in front of the judge against Mr. Fred. So, the win rate if Mr. Fred was the plaintiff attorney was 100%. If Mr. Fred was the defendant in the case, the win rate was 98%. All of the other attorney firms tested against this judge showed a win rate of between 40-45%. The contrast was profound.

I know that my attorney had had enough of the judge; I'm not really sure what started her thinking about what she would propose to me. She wasn't aware early on that I was researching data until she became concerned why Mr. Fred continued to use his legislative privilege to delay the recusal hearing. Since Mr. Fred had the outcome won anyway, she could see no reason for Mr. Fred to continue to delay.

I'd called her to ask why there was yet another lag in our case. It was when we finally talked, and she found out that I'd been analyzing Mr. Fred's cases, that her interest was piqued. She made a few calls to the courthouse. What was happening is that the clerks who were Mr. Fred's operatives in the courthouse had reported to Mr. Fred my showing up and getting copies of his case records.

Mr. Fred knew that he was exposed. He'd done what he could to delay the case because he feared what I was "up to". My attorney proposed that I present the data set in the recusal hearing. She said not to expect a positive outcome, though, and that Judge Malinda *never* ruled against Mr. Fred. But it was our only chance to get a recusal from the judge, who would certainly rule for Chuck.

I arrived at the courthouse, briefcase in hand, and Mr. Fred sneered at me. I was called to the stand. I presented the facts that we were requesting a recusal because our data indicated that no one ever won against Mr. Fred. Mr. Fred started raising his voice, questioning me, and saying that I did not know what I was doing. Chuck was there as well, staring at me, oblivious to the fact that his attorney had proposed to sell him out completely in very recent weeks. I defended the fact that any citizen can look at prior court outcomes for their own education and benefit and that these were public records. I could tell that Mr. Fred was truly caught off balance.

Mr. Fred tried to accuse me of plotting the entire delay that he himself had orchestrated with his legislative privilege. He accused me of many things that were easily put aside by my attorney's objections. Then he tried his final move at the urging of Chuck, whispering in his ear. There was an email Chuck had sent me related to our new child support deal. This was an email I'd received earlier that year, back when there was hope that Chuck would actually do what he said. I told Mr. Fred yes, that this email had looked promising, but that his firm had sent me an unsignable document that didn't address tuition or insurance at all, and that Chuck had simply abruptly stopped paying support without disclosing anything necessary for a negotiated settlement.

Mr. Fred was not happy; it had become clear that in the depths of his attacks on me, that Chuck had been lying to him as well. The characters in this drama were much like a Three Stooges-like botched episode of dimwit thugs in three distinct mugshots: Jessica, who had unethically disclosed my private business to both Mr. Fred and one of my friends; Mr. Fred, the manipulative and corrupt politician; and Chuck, who had built his own house of cards with his continued lies.

At the end of the case, Judge Malinda stated that the judge would not recuse, in spite of the data I presented. I know that my attorney presented a terrific closing argument about appearances of bias. If I had another judge, I would have had nothing to fear as Chuck was now in his third contempt related to support. My own thinking is that Judge Malinda may have given Mr. Fred a tongue lashing later about being more careful in the future and putting her in a hot spot.

My attorney thanked the judge for her decision, looked at me and said, "No surprise there." Chuck disappeared quickly from the room, no doubt wanting to avoid his own attorney after being caught in yet another series of lies, and Mr. Fred stormed away, having not achieved the testimony that he wanted. But our last chance for justice had been exhausted.

My Second Escape

My relocation request was never heard. Mr. Fred kept stalling my case, and Ren was torn about moving, since he was in high school and had many friends. Chuck continued to lie. In the end, Chuck was still in contempt of court, and therefore would theoretically have to satisfy his own contempt issues before addressing his child support change filing. I perceived that Mr. Fred wasn't thrilled with Chuck after finding out he'd lied again.

I'd already sold all my furniture in an estate sale and moved out of my rent house into a temporary furnished apartment for the last month of hearings. Ren really enjoyed that space because it was close to town and he could walk to town to get a burger. It was magical how God provided us that peaceful time together in the face of the awful storm going on. I still held out hope that Ren would be able to accompany me. Still, I had to give the situation to God as my entire safety net had fallen out from under me.

The morning I left, Ren was crying. I wanted to cry but couldn't. I'd cried my heart out for years. We'd exhausted every legal avenue to get a fair shake in court. By that time, over the last 8 years, Cody had spent over $56k defending my rights and my children's rights. That is the exact amount that it cost in fertility treatments to eventually get pregnant with Gray and Ren. So $112k later, I'd delivered Chuck his children, and then defended my rights as their biological mother. By then, Ren had been in counseling, and had a ready counselor available to him, a driver's license and use of a car, and was taller than Chuck. He had already confronted Chuck on a number of issues. He was strong and resilient, and I trusted that despite how crazy the circumstances were, that I was doing the only thing God would let me do at the time.

I wheeled my suitcase into the airport, speaking with Gray by phone. He said to me, "Mom, you sound good." I couldn't imagine how I was still upright and walking, or how my head was up. I'd had an immediate family death in the middle of all this, and I'd spent hours and hours driving and crying. I'd cried it all out. It was a grayish, rainy fall day. When the airplane wheels went up, I did shed a tear of exhaustion and concern for Ren, and sadness that my life had come to this, after doing what was right for the children for so long.

I can't explain what happened to me when I got off the plane in my new state. I'd grabbed my suitcase from the upper compartment in the plane and expected to curl up in a ball in my closet for days. I walked out into the concourse. It was sunny and busy. The air was dry and crisp. People were running around talking, smiling, and enjoying their travel as they moved through the terminal. In the corner of my eye, a young woman with a hippie-style outfit strolled past me. The airport was a hodgepodge of freedom. In that moment, these words materialized in my head like a cinema marquee. Suddenly, I heard my heart exclaim: "I have just divorced Chuck for the last time!" And I knew that I had.

Summation

When I went through my divorce with Chuck, I never saw a decade of harassment coming. I imagined that it would be ugly at first, because he was an angry person even in happier days in our marriage. When Ren and Gray began to be affected, it surprised me, because it never occurred to me that Chuck would take out his wrath on them.

After the first phony case, I realized how right my first attorney was about my having the "wrong color car". The next several years created a form of PTSD for me; a hypervigilant state in which I was second guessing every move I made. It started a negative phase of "parenting in fear" since anything I said or did could result in a court case, no matter how right I was. Then came the anaphylactic stage, in which I would literally feel myself choking in the middle of the night, almost immediately before some new action would occur.

Even though this memoir stops at the point that I arrived at the airport after escaping Chuck's continued court wrath, his efforts to pursue me still did not stop. My new attorney told me months and months later that Chuck continued to try to incite legal action, even after he'd won everything there was to win. I'd learned by that time that it was better to stay quiet and let Ren grow up and get his own life than it was to "poke the bear".

In the end, my life changed for the worse when my judge changed, and nothing I could count on before applied.

No amount of money or good behavior would ever change the outcome in a court that is decided before you get there. No overt violation in support mattered in the end, since the legislator attorney could delay cases indefinitely.

No parent or child should have to worry about business or political relationships, or "paying off" a GAL, to gain a positive outcome in a family court case. No judge should be allowed to practice who shows bias, over and over, in any court of law. Most predominantly, my fervent plea is that "the least of these" (that is, victim families) should be afforded the very **BEST** ethics in family courts.

To reiterate, my directive in writing this book was to 1) provide a soothing catharsis for anyone going through emotional or court abuse at any level, and 2) to suggest avenues for change based on what we have learned in decades of malfunction in the family court systems. The following chapters are collections of spiritual insights, recent news, and pathways for change. Additionally, there are some reference materials which may be helpful to you in your journey. This information is also on our web: (**www.roadtoelroi.com**).

Chapter 2: Spiritual Relevance

My Journey as a Handmaiden

The following piece by Rabbi Jonathan Kligler spoke to me with clarity about the conditions under which Hagar was required to function in the patriarchal society of her time in which slavery was the accepted norm. Modern assisted reproductive technologies have simply provided a more arms-length method of achieving children, but with the same end game. Sarah wanted to please Abraham, and so she "gave" Hagar to him for the purpose of producing a child. Hagar, "The Stranger" was doing her job as a slave. It is no surprise to anyone that these relationships caused extreme conflict.

This drama Hagar was caught up in ultimately spawned a nation, and her story serves to remind us of the magnitude of strength innately present in motherhood. Moreover, how society treats the weak foretells how we will eventually be treated, as history continues to prove over and over. What the story ultimately says to me is that El Roi, *The God Who Sees*, always sees me, no matter how marginalized or inconsequential my life may seem. I have felt the curious emotional distance of "The Stranger" by being in a situation in which I carried and bore a stranger's child. But I did not feel safe to speak of it; to speak my Truth.

After God gifted me astounding children full of hope, promise, and worth, the corrupt and arrogant system years later would attempt to squelch them from knowing their own Truth.

Still, God saw us, by the evidence of our finding life-changing relationships -- an oasis in a desert of oppression from our Truth.

Rabbi Jonathan's words on Hagar, combined with the illumination gained from a random retreat on a random day, I was graced by a radiant spiritual light that made sense of my years of wandering. This flame was accompanied with a directive to tell my story for the benefit of victims of narcissistic abuse. The following brilliant analogy in the following section that Rabbi Jonathan produced after his own illumination challenges us to look beyond traditional thinking.

What is even more poignant is the objectification of the mother-child relationship for purposes of control and ownership, and how modern Hagar's story feels to those of us who have experienced warfare involving children. There are many in our family of victims who will readily relate to being thrown out in the wilderness. My own reflections about story of Hagar, Sarah, and Abraham would raise an eyebrow, but I won't pretend to know the mind of God.

What Hagar went through isn't a depiction of the weakness and imperfection of God; it speaks to the fallibility of being human.

Sarah and Abraham couldn't wait for God's promise, so they used Hagar to achieve parenthood, yet God worked with that recipe for disaster to build two great nations. Hagar gained her freedom and saved her son; but not without great pain along the way.

Hagar The Stranger
by Rabbi Jonathan Kligler

Turn it and turn it, for everything is in it, Ben Bag Bag taught about studying the Torah. Reflect on it, pore over it, grow old and gray with it, for there is no better reward than this. Well, I'm not gray yet, but I sure am getting older, and bald already happened. And with age maybe I'm starting to repeat myself more, but I'll tell you again: Ben Bag Bag, the ancient sage with the best alliterative name, was a wise man. The Torah continues to reveal its deep wisdom to me, and ever-greater connecting patterns of meaning unfold before me. It turns out that the Torah's major themes, its central messages, reverberate throughout the text, like themes and variations in a symphony. The more attuned I become to a great symphony, the more awed I become by the genius of the composer, and ever more uplifted. So it is that as I embrace the genius of the Torah, its great moral themes resound and reverberate in unanticipated and compelling ways.

In the special Torah reading assigned for the first day of Rosh Hashanah we are thrust into the drama of the life of Abraham and Sarah and their family, Hagar the Egyptian maidservant and her son Ishmael, and Sarah's miracle baby Isaac. Every year we return to these 21 verses, and to our "first family." This year I find myself drawn to Hagar, for I noticed something that I am sure many have noticed before me, but I only saw it for the first time. All names are meaningful and symbolic in the Torah, although some of the meanings have become lost to us across the millennia. Because the Torah is written without vowels, it is possible to pronounce the words in multiple ways, and this is a key to finding implied meanings. So, the name Hagar can also be read ha-ger, the stranger, the foreigner, the Other. Then, instead of "Hagar hamitzrit," Hagar the Egyptian, we read "Ha-ger hamitzrit," the stranger from Egypt. Hagar is now no longer merely an individual character, she is the first appearance of perhaps the key archetype of the Torah: the stranger. And she becomes the first example of one of the Torah's great questions: How do we treat the stranger?

The Torah is an ongoing call to moral responsibility. When Cain kills his brother Abel, and then asks defiantly, "Am I my brother's keeper?" his question resounds to this day. But for me what raises the Torah to the sublime is that it is not satisfied with the imperative of caring for one's kin. The Torah insists that the well being of the stranger is our responsibility, too. The well being of the stranger is a much more difficult assignment to grasp, let alone to care about. There is an obvious self-interest in caring about our kin: we need them to also care about us. But the stranger? What possible interest might we have in the stranger? Yet our Torah insists that we regard the stranger with as much concern as we regard our own. It begins with the fundamental premise of Genesis, that every human is created in the image of the divine, and builds its moral case from there. Then, the Torah places as its central narrative our own experience as strangers, oppressed in the land of Egypt. We cry out, and the Creator hears our cry, the cry of the powerless. And because we are created in the divine image, we are forever after called upon to emulate our Creator, and therefore to hear the cry of the powerless. The Torah repeats the instruction to care for the stranger at least 33 times, far more than any other commandment in the Torah. It seems to me that when a rule is repeated over and over and over again, it is not only because it is important, it is because people are having trouble following the instruction! We are terrible at following the instruction of caring for the stranger. Again, what's in it for us? And so, God calls upon us repeatedly to develop empathy: do not oppress the stranger, for you know the feelings of the stranger, having yourselves been strangers in the land of Egypt.

How do we develop empathy? How do we identify with the powerless, whom the Torah typically refers to as the stranger, the slave, the orphan, and the widow?

Which brings us back to Hagar. She is the first stranger in the Torah. She is also a maidservant, a slave. And she is an Egyptian. In the worldview of the Torah, the harmful actions we perpetrate upon others invariably redound back upon us. Many readers have wondered about the cruelty of this story: after Sarah's son Isaac is weaned, Sarah sees Ishmael, Hagar's son, laughing or playing with Isaac, and she says to Abraham, "Get rid of this servant and her son!" Sarah seems petty, Abraham passive, and worst of all, God tells Abraham to do as Sarah says! But this is more than an ancient family drama with an inscrutable deity making capricious demands. The treatment that Abraham and Sarah perpetrate upon Hagar the Egyptian and her son Ishmael sets into motion the events that will eventually lead the descendants of Abraham's other son Isaac to become strangers and slaves themselves in the land of Egypt. And without our sojourn in Egypt, our people's deepest wisdom, our mature empathy, could never have been formed.

Remember, the Torah is about each of us. That is why we are still studying it. And when I examine my life, I am always faced with the fact that whatever wisdom I have distilled from this roller coaster of life is a result of lessons learned from my suffering. We look back on our lives, and sometimes we are able to say, you know if I hadn't had to get clean, or been through that illness, or had to deal with my crazy parent, I might never have learned compassion, or understood humility, or found my voice... Or, as the Torah puts it, "remember the long road on which YHVH, Life Unfolding, led you these 40 years in the wilderness, in order to test you, to find out what was in your hearts." Recently I was complimenting a friend who had given me good advice. I said, "How did you get so wise?" She hesitated and laughed, and then I answered for her and said: "Oh, I know: the hard way!" Or as the Torah puts it, we were forged in the blast furnace of Egypt, the hard way. We pray for the strength, courage, faith, and plain old luck not to be crushed by our struggles, but to learn and grow from them.

Our story also introduces the central element of the Jewish understanding of God. It is not an assertion that can be proven, yet the Torah assumes it is so: YHVH, the Creator, hears the cry of the oppressed and the powerless, and is with them. When Moses first encounters YHVH at the burning bush, and asks, "Who am I that I should go to Pharaoh and free the Children of Israel from Egypt?" (Ex. 3:11) God does not exhort Moses that Moses is up to the job. Rather God promises to be with Moses: "And God said, 'I will be with you – ehyeh imach – that shall be your sign that it was I who sent you." (Ex. 3:12) In the next verse Moses asks what is God's name, in case the people ask Moses who sent him. God reveals the name Ehyeh-Asher-Ehyeh (I will be that I will be), and then adds "Thus shall you say to the Children of Israel: 'Ehyeh sent me to you!' (Ex. 3:14) So, one of God's names is Ehyeh, "I Will Be," and it echoes the previous verse, "I will be with you!" We might say that one of God's names, and certainly one God's attributes, is I Will Be With You.

When Hagar and Ishmael are cast out into the wilderness, and the lad is dying of thirst and crying, Hagar goes and sits a bowshot away so that she will not have to listen to the cries of the child as he perishes, and she weeps. "And God heard the cry of the boy, and an angel of God called to Hagar from heaven and said: What troubles you Hagar? Do not fear! For God has heard the cry of the boy in the place where he is." In the Torah, the stranger is usually included in a grouping with the widow and the orphan. In the ancient agricultural and patriarchal clan society of Israel, these were the truly powerless: the stranger had no land holding, and no protector, and neither did the widow or the orphan (referring here to a child without a father). The stranger, the orphan, and the widow, and also the slave, had no political power or legal recourse. They were truly at the mercy of others. In our story, Hagar and Ishmael embody all aspects of this powerless condition: Hagar is a stranger, a slave, and effectively a widow, her son an orphan. And God hears their cry. Ishmael's name means "God hears," just as God's name means "I will be with you."

If we are created in the Divine image, then we must find in ourselves the capacity for mercy, the capacity to hear the cry of the powerless and to respond with care.

Throughout the Torah, whenever we are called upon to care for the disenfranchised and the stranger, there is no direct consequence that is threatened if we do not. For what can the powerless do to us? Instead the Torah can only assert relentlessly that God hears the cries of the powerless, that we should revere and be in awe of God, and that therefore we should also have mercy upon them, for we were once powerless in the land of Egypt. Does God hear their cry? I honestly don't know. But I cherish my tradition that insists that in order to fulfill our destiny as human beings we need to hear and respond to the cry of the weak. Perhaps, as many before me have suggested, the God of righteousness and justice exists, but only in potential. Perhaps it is only through our own righteous and compassionate actions that the glory of God becomes manifest in the world.

This teaching reaches its pinnacle in the very center of the Torah, Parshat Kedoshim in the Book of Vayikra, Leviticus. The parshah begins with the familiar call to emulate the divine "You shall be holy, for I YHVH your God am holy." The instructions then climax with verse 19, "Love your neighbor as yourself." This is the Golden Rule, the heart of the Torah. But remember the saying I began with: "Turn it and turn it for everything is in it"? I have always focused on verse 19, for what could be more central to our quest? But one day, I turned the Torah a bit and verse 33 lit up before me: "When a stranger dwells with you in your land, do not oppress him. Treat the stranger like a fellow citizen; you shall love the stranger as yourself, for you were strangers in the land of Egypt. I am YHVH your God."

V'ahavta et ha-ger kamocha. Love the stranger as yourself. Our Torah gives us two explicit commands: Love your neighbor as yourself, and love the stranger as yourself. The Torah's grasp of human nature is complete. We know intuitively that loving our neighbor as ourselves, difficult as that might be, is in our own interest. Any social group thrives when its members take each other's interests to heart, when we curb selfishness in favor of a common good. But the injunction to love the stranger as yourself asks us to rise to an even higher level: there is no consequence to us if the stranger is ignored. We turn our eyes toward them simply because they are God's children. To love the stranger represents an outrageous leap out of the typical moral economy, in which we do kindnesses and expect to be repaid in kind. In loving the stranger, we transcend self-interest.

This is the demand of Judaism: to rise above our nature and create a new way of being. In an earlier time, when communities were smaller and self-contained, this holy task was more limited, for the stranger was by definition someone who had wandered into your community. The law did not pertain to an unknown soul in another land. That task of inclusion was difficult enough, which is perhaps why the Torah repeats the command three dozen times. Today the challenge is multiplied exponentially. We live in a world in which we can call a technical help line and find ourselves speaking with someone in India – or Mauritius, as happened to me recently! We live in a world in which it becomes clearer, shall I say starker, almost daily that our individual fates are intertwined, whether we would like them to be or not. We live in a nation that was built on the premise that a society could be built of strangers, each given inalienable rights. A songwriter named Betsy Rose wrote the lyric: "We may have come here in different ships, but we're in the same boat now." Never has the commandment to treat the stranger as one of your own been more pressing. But that doesn't make it any easier, only more urgent.

There is, as we know, only one place to practice this radical demand of empathy. Right here, right now, in the place where you are. Our high-minded ideas of the unity of the planet are not worth the paper we write them on if we do not enact our principles where we live. So rather than drawing a tight circle that includes the people we know and leaves others on the outside, let's draw as big a circle as we can around us that includes not just Sarah and Isaac, but Hagar and Ishmael, the stranger, the weak, the newcomer, the odd, the gentile, the Jew who doesn't think he or she belongs, the people we just plain disagree with, the other. Even if it makes us uncomfortable some of the time. Even if we're not very good at it. For in so doing we will be fulfilling the highest aspiration of our tradition – we will be realizing our divine nature.

Julia Boylan shared a famous verse with me when I was discussing these questions a few weeks ago. I'll close with it. It is called "Outwitted" by Edwin Markham:

He drew a circle that shut me out –
Heretic, rebel, a thing to flout.
But Love and I had the wit to win:
We drew a circle that took him in!

May we all draw that big circle in our lives this year, drawing others into it with love. And remember, whenever you draw a circle around you, you are at the center. That is where change begins. You have my love, support, and total encouragement to draw your circle wide, and to know that you are a vessel for making the divine promise of empathy manifest in the world. L'SHANA TOVA TIKATEIVU.

Where in the World Is King Solomon?

1 Kings 3:16-28 New King James Version (NKJV)

[16] Now two women *who were* harlots came to the king, and stood before him. [17] And one woman said, "O my lord, this woman and I dwell in the same house; and I gave birth while she *was* in the house. [18] Then it happened, the third day after I had given birth, that this woman also gave birth. And we *were* together; [a]no one *was* with us in the house, except the two of us in the house. [19] And this woman's son died in the night, because she lay on him. [20] So she arose in the middle of the night and took my son from my side, while your maidservant slept, and laid him in her bosom, and laid her dead child in my bosom. [21] And when I rose in the morning to nurse my son, there he was, dead. But when I had examined him in the morning, indeed, he was not my son whom I had borne."

[22] Then the other woman said, "No! But the living one *is* my son, and the dead one *is* your son."

And the first woman said, "No! But the dead one *is* your son, and the living one *is* my son."

Thus they spoke before the king.

[23] And the king said, "The one says, 'This *is* my son, who lives, and your son *is* the dead one'; and the other says, 'No! But your son *is* the dead one, and my son *is* the living one.'" [24] Then the king said, "Bring me a sword." So they brought a sword before the king. [25] And the king said, "Divide the living child in two, and give half to one, and half to the other."

[26] Then the woman whose son *was* living spoke to the king, for she yearned with compassion for her son; and she said, "O my lord, give her the living child, and by no means kill him!"

But the other said, "Let him be neither mine nor yours, *but* divide *him*."
²⁷ So the king answered and said, "Give the first woman the living child, and by no means kill him; she *is* his mother."
²⁸ And all Israel heard of the judgment which the king had rendered; and they feared the king, for they saw that the wisdom of God *was* in him to administer justice.

When Solomon was presented with these two women who likely didn't pay their attorneys thousands to play cat and mouse games with each other for months, he hadn't just come from a European vacation or had to kowtow to his political supporters at a $200 a plate dinner. What I'm saying is that Solomon had the levity to rely on his own personal insight and wisdom to render a judgement. To even a total fool, the woman who declared that the child must live, even if given to the other woman, was the one who truly loved the child.

But Solomon doesn't exist in the modern-day family court system, because Solomon, if living today:

- As a judge, Solomon might have been trained not to believe either woman in the courtroom.

- He would have been more likely to rule for the woman with the best attorney or the one he had the most politically prolific relationship with.

- To preserve his livelihood, he would also have to pay attention to the political winds of trade in his district, who's who, and powerful forces that could help or hurt him down the road.

- The women's attorneys would have had 4-inch-thick swaths of code law to delay, continue, or confound the issue, further draining whatever funds the women had.

- They would each be allowed to make up whatever story they wanted without fear of being punished for lying in family courts, since the family courts generally don't care about perjury.

- DNA would have been ordered and clearly identified who the mother was, and all they would have ended up on Jerry Springer or the Dr. Phil Show.

Now, I'm not trying to be funny, I'm just stating the obvious: Solomon couldn't exhibit the judgment skills in a modern-day family court he had back then, because of the system we have now. How do we get back to truth and justice? I reviewed two different academic papers on Solomon's historical judgment, which has been a backbone of beginning law school courses for hundreds of years. One of the papers questioned the 'real mother' theory of Solomon's actions, suggesting that perhaps the real mother may have been the one who insisted on killing the child (with the input of real law students).

The other scholarly paper focused on how women were objectified in the day of Solomon, and how the sword he drew represents the abortion of female representation and male control over reproductive freedoms. With obtuse analyses like these, it is no wonder that our entire legal system has suffered a loss of basic reasoning!

I've pondered this issue of change for an exceedingly long time, and devised a preliminary skeletal framework that I feel would encourage transparency and honesty in the system, along with better outcomes for our children:

- ***It is my belief that Family Court judges perhaps shouldn't be elected, but that a hybrid should be proposed.***

There are some <u>great</u> elected judges out there, but making judges into political animals forces them to always preserve their positions. It causes them to have a tendency to be concerned when one of their big donors walks into their courtroom in a custody case, especially when campaign fundraising is coming up. The decisions that affect their supporters' personal lives will loom larger than life in their next election cycle. This disadvantages regular parents, such as stay-at-home moms who aren't "important" people.

- ***I believe that full data disclosure on outcomes, rulings, data, and statistics in family court should be available.***

This would include statistics on which attorneys fare better in specific courtrooms, whether more male or female attorneys prevail, whether male or female litigants prevail more frequently, and other relevant facts. While some litigation research software yields access to cases and outcomes, this information is not readily available to the public.

- ***The selection of judges should be based on experience-driven and/or peer-influenced appointments.***

Mediators or court officers should be tried, tested, and proven, ethically-sound family court warhorses who are above reproach. This could be achieved by structuring the appointment and renewals of their terms based on strong peer review, outcomes, and positive feedback from constituents.

- ***Family code has to change state by state.***

Federal mandates on family law codes could recommend change; however, individual states will need to revise and modernize family court codes. These modifications include eliminating parental alienation terminology as a method of removing custody, firm guidelines on what is considered "change of circumstances", and actually enforcing child support violation penalties. Lying under oath in Family Court should carry penalties.

- ***Domestic violence has to start being taken seriously.***

Stalking and violation of protection orders, including verifiable domestic abuse, should carry with them restriction of access to children unless under police supervision. If a spouse has physically harmed the other parent, they are capable of hurting their own children. Child murder statistics collected by the Center for Judicial Excellence (**www.centerforjudicialexcellence.com**) prove this beyond the shadow of a doubt.

- ***Judge education must be revamped to match up with what is really going on in the area of emotional, financial, and narcissistic abuse.***

Training judges to disbelieve women who claim physical abuse during an attempt to escape a marriage is completely insane, since this is the time that women are at the most risk. Judges should have discernment, although evidence should be required in any abuse allegation. Children should be believed and not punished for speaking out.

- ***Family court should have the highest ethical standards in practice and participants.***

Ethics in family court should be more stringent than in any other venue. GALs or custody evaluators caught taking payoffs should be prosecuted at the highest levels. Judicial councils evaluating unethical practices reported should be held accountable for fully investigating each claim and following through with witnesses, testimonies, and fact-finding. Judges should not routinely get away with actions that cause harm to innocents.

- ***Screening processes for vexatious litigation would help lower the instance of post-separation and post-divorce harassment.***

A pattern of court stalking is not difficult to see once a party has filed multiple cases. These patterns are highly identifiable from both a filing and evidence of abuse history. Although this point is listed last, it is probably the easiest to implement. Severe penalties should accompany intentional court abuse (domestic abuse by proxy).

At the very least, a vexatious litigator should be required pay his or her victim's court costs, along with a stiff fine.

The Isolation That Narcissistic Abuse Creates

I'm not sure nonvictims can fully understand the depth of isolation that occurs during a battle with a vengeful abuser. Social, financial, and legal harassment, and even estrangement from one's own family happens. A sad but common phenomenon is a demented ex managing to turn blood relatives of a victim into enemies through lies.

I remember after my divorce, people I barely knew would come up to me saying "You're back!" and I would say, "What?" and they would tell me about how I moved to another state. I'd been in the same town for over 30 years, with Ren and Gray. Once the boys were with me in a restaurant, and a woman came up to the table who recognized them and went on to tell me how I'd lived an interesting life, and moved out of state, and that she used to cut Chuck's hair. Now why would Chuck bother to spin a tale about me to his hairdresser? I have to admit, I was secretly relieved to have this happen in front of Ren and Gray.

What people uneducated in this type of clinical dysfunction (Narcissistic Personality Disorder, or NPD) don't realize is that attackers will not only lie, they will go to extremes, often skillfully, to manufacture falsified evidence, recruit others to corroborate their stories, and bait victims to react in ways that will further convince relatives and friends. These actions go on sometimes for years, imprisoning their victim in a cloak of false social positioning.

Unfortunately, narcissists will "set up" each person in their manufactured drama: in church, they are a financially giving, spiritual, and caring committee member. At work, they can be successful, driven, and intelligent. To loyal friends, they are the victim: their target mistreated them and now they are devastated. No manner of proof or convincing will dissuade the narcissist's loyal minions.

The personal experience of the "target" with the narcissist will always be in sharp contrast to how others are treated. Just like a little girl whose pigtails are pulled daily by a bully at school, many times the teachers don't want to deal with discipline in the schools or calling out behaviors. If the bullied child speaks out, then she too is punished. The teacher will tell the bullied child to "work it out". This leaves the young victim even more isolated. The bully, knowing he or she will not be punished for his/her actions, is emboldened by the inaction of the authority figure (in this case the teacher; in later years, her family court judge) and involves other classmates in alienating or further injuring the little girl.

The harassed child is bewildered and eventually decides (since her idea of right and wrong is now turned upside down) that it is SHE who is faulty and inadequate, and that _she_ has caused the bully to act this way. This is how the cycle of narcissistic abuse begins. There is a fine line between jerk and sociopath. It is taken far too lightly when this pathology shows up during youth. All we need do is substitute judges for teachers and we can see exactly the scenario that occurs when a narcissist wants revenge in an untrained courtroom.

Mean People and Busybodies

If it wasn't bad enough already with the corruption I faced in my case, I had a busybody mucking up my situation. In her arrogance, she inserted herself without my asking, into my case. To make it worse, my husband and I had paid her firm thousands for representation using their other attorneys. She took it upon herself to unethically call Chuck's attorney and disclose private things that were going on in my life that I'd confided in her.

Chuck's attorney couldn't be trusted in front of the Pope himself and he continued to file cases for Chuck despite his promises to Jessica to "help" us. Jessica told others outside client confidentiality about my case, further embarrassing me and hurting my situation. With "friends" like this, who needs enemies?

Be very careful who you disclose personal information to about your case or situation. In my case, I thought this woman was a real friend. But, if I'd held my discussion parameters closer to the vest and limited to only those close friends and family that had proven over time to be loyal, reliable and ethical, my case would not have been compromised to such a degree.

If you find yourself in a situation in which there is professional misconduct, you always will have the option of filing an ethical complaint with that state's ethics board or disciplinary board. In my state, action is almost always limited to attorneys stealing money from escrow accounts, or other overt violations. Only a very small percentage of attorneys are actually disciplined, and usually the price is paid by the plaintiff in being blacklisted by other attorneys.

I saved pages and pages of texts and emails related to Jessica's representation of the relationship with Mr. Fred, but there was no real mechanism to remedy what happened, since the courts and ethics boards are so ineffectual in my state. In order to bring you a story that is just and right, I had to walk away from anything untoward, and fight for the truth. This culminated in my data collection on court cases that cost me countless hours, for which I had to pay for legal representation to be able to present.

Flying Monkeys

If you hadn't already heard the term 'flying monkeys' then I will explain: the name was derived from *The Wizard of Oz*, in which the wicked witch employs the flying varmints to attack Dorothy and her tagalongs. The flying monkeys simply do as the witch says without question and act immediately on her behalf. Their sheer numbers and zombie-like dissonance is disturbing, and the witch cackles diabolically, *"Release the monkeys!"*

I think it is important for emotional abuse victims to be familiar with the term, because it can be a solace in realizing that psychology recognizes group bullying and narcissistic targeting through others as a tool of abuse. When Chuck threatened to have 'the whole team' testify against me in court (because everyone hated me, of course) and I had to pay my attorney to debunk that, there was a double whammy of flying monkeys. Chuck had apparently turned (in his mind) the whole Lacrosse team into flying monkeys, and then he'd turned his attorney into a flying monkey as well.

Of course, I was bewildered, because he had maybe two friends who were parents on the team that I suspected could be in cahoots against me. I was friends with some of the moms on the team, and I can't imagine that they would have had negative things to say about me, especially to the degree that they would show up in court to say how awful of a person I was. The larger-than-life claims that Chuck would make would still hit their mark in intimidating me and making my life miserable, and for a while, I believed that many people did indeed dislike me.

When I look back on it all now, it seems trivial; but back then, I was so mentally exhausted from the "Chuck War" that everything seemed so monumental.

Another notable time Chuck used flying monkeys is when he used his attorney to tell my attorney that Gray did not want to live with me anymore. This was a direct blow to my parenthood, and an attempt at bullying his way out of having to be responsible for his ignoring of court orders. By then, I was educated on his pathology and hit him between the eyes by telling Gray, who was a teenager, that he could go live wherever he wanted. It was then that Chuck's lies became exposed and he began to lose credibility.

When I look at the concept of flying monkeys squarely, I go mentally back to high school. In my school, there were popular cliques. If you did not drink, make out, or do things that were otherwise 'cool' then you were a dork, and you had flying monkeys. The fact that I had a lot of loving Christian friends really led me astray later, as I learned in my adulthood that not everyone who attends church is a friend.

This led to even further delusion when 'shrew-woman' showed up at my home late at night to scream at me about her life and how everyone thought I was pathetic, when I hadn't said anything to her negatively. This woman, if I had to guess, was a bully in high school. She'd been having a bad time, and I did not know she was about to go through a divorce. She simply decided to come to my house and unload that night. If she hadn't threatened to 'ruin me' if I told anyone what she said, I would have marked it up to a random occurrence. Now I am convinced that I am a narcissist magnet.

Any mental image that can help you compartmentalize what is happening and acceptance that flying monkeys are "evil spirits" in your spiritual war, is helpful to your healing.

Just one kind word from anyone any given day released so much of my stress and worry and gave me strength. I don't want to sound like a Pollyanna or do-gooder, but I believe that one of the reasons I've been charged with this book is to reach out to you and ask you to be one of the strong ones; be the one who is sensitive enough to realize that there are victims all around you.

Be perceptive, kind, and full of love, and be the person who says something genuinely caring. Commit yourself that you will never be a flying monkey, and that you will be a beacon of light for others affected by this thief of life psychologists call narcissistic personality disorder.

Some of the other terms I've heard are the terms "friendlies" and "unfriendlies". My friend Ariana has laid that term like a visual label on the foreheads of those she's classified. This is helpful for her in terms of her emotional toolbox to quickly categorize her next conversation with them, which for unfriendlies will be factual, to the point, and short, if she must engage at all. Or, more deviously, to plant information that will confound the narcissist if repeated back.

The main flying monkey that a narcissist can employ is always going to be their super-fly monkey, which is sometimes their new supply or spouse. When a spouse is employed to be a flying monkey, I have derived a more apt term. Because the "monkey" is now tied to the narcissist legally, they become an organ grinding monkey. If you've seen these performers, the handler will play the music and the monkey will dance and collect coins. In the same way, the organ grinding monkey spouse will "dance" to whatever tune the narcissist plays, and the story then becomes so much more enchanting.

Crazy Making

One of Ariana's ex's first legal harassment actions (domestic abuse by proxy) was to claim that she was insane using family court filings that required she go through psychological testing. A person of strong faith who had served as a missionary, with a degree and solid career in hospital administration, Ariana is the furthest from "crazy" that a person can get. She is a nurturing, emotionally intelligent mother of two, with throngs of friends and a huge extended family. There is nothing in her history at all to indicate instability. In fact, it is Gilbert, her ex, who has been a loose cannon, causing chaos and misery everywhere he goes.

While this effort on the part of a narcissist sounds rare in family court, it isn't. What Gilbert was trying to do is actually "break her" by employing the abuse that the filing itself caused. This is more aptly described as "throwing something up against the wall to see if it sticks". Ariana had to be evaluated and tested, call witnesses, and have her case usurped by "scheduling" changes in court, even though she had a preferentially set court date. She had to pay through the nose to prove that she wasn't insane, and then pay to have that conclusion presented in court.

Was Gilbert held accountable in any way by the court for his false attacks? **No!** It was Ariana, her parents who helped fund her defense, and her children who have paid, on a long-term basis. That initial action put her at a disadvantage financially throughout the rest of her post-divorce life of continual court and personal harassment. If courts were run appropriately, a filer would be required to have legitimate evidence of a parent being unstable before even thinking about legal action.

When Chuck decided to try to take control of Ren and Gray away from me to stop them from knowing their genetics, "crazy" is where they went first. My attorney received a letter from Mr. Fred, implying that I was unstable, and addressing my mental health. What wasn't known by either attorney is that my biological mother committed suicide when I was 12. Chuck knew this was a trigger for me, and he used that to bully and demean me on purpose.

When Gilbert filed his case against Ariana, he was actually counting on his actions causing enough damage to make her crack or completely fall apart, creating a self-actualization that is very commonly incited by malignant narcissists. It is no wonder why actions such as these cause PTSD.

It is relatively simple for courts to identify phony filing patterns and unfounded claims of vengeful parents (see Narcissistic Identifier flowcharts in this book pages 231-232). Why aren't the courts more proactive? I believe the answers lie in these areas: 1) lack of accountability and unwillingness to take a bold stance out of either laziness or "default" boilerplate determinations 2) the money machine of financial opportunity for court professionals, and 3) the nature of the state codes, which readily allow for "one hand not being responsible for the other" along with the ServPro® effect of expungement, where prior history cannot be used against a chronic abuser.

Official labeling of family court harassment needs to align with what it actually is: **domestic abuse**. Until that happens, the fate of victims and their children will be subject to whatever direction the wind blows in the courtroom or in the mind of the predator. Our children deserve better, and we already know enough through data and outcomes that a plan to cancel this blank check that has been available to batterers is desperately needed.

The Millstone

Nothing that I have ever come across spiritually while I've crawled through this long journey of court and emotional abuse, has been more poignant related to children than the analogy of the millstone. This admonishment addresses the Evil One who would lead a child astray from God. For the children murdered to date because of court failures, the system as an inanimate "cause" will not take the spiritual blame for what an individual in power allowed to happen when he or she had the authority to stop it, and didn't:

Matthew 18:5-9
"Whoever receives one such child in my name receives me, but whoever causes one of these little ones who believe in me to sin, it would be better for him to have a great millstone fastened around his neck and to be drowned in the depth of the sea."

Tens of millions of children who cannot ever fulfill their God given purposes have been derailed from who they were supposed to be because of adult self-interests and power grabs. For this reason, I feel that the lesson of The Millstone is an ominous prediction offered by Christ for what is going on in our court systems.

This form of self-absorbed vigilantism on the part of batterers, by making children and parents "pay" for escaping their sad, phony version of love is destroying our culture. Court failures have led to murders of children, suicides, loss of incomes, and wholesale losses of relationships of children with their loving parents. A host of grieving grandparents has also had to live their lives watching a living hell.

I believe, depending on the degree of the pathology, that narcissism is Evil itself: Satan, the one we dread in the middle of the night. I believe in the polarity of light vs. darkness, and there is no better example of the embodiment of abuse than that of taking a child's love from a parent out of anger or revenge.

We are all responsible for children who cannot embrace their purpose or feel loved because of an adult's selfish pursuits. Narcissism is an evil spirit that swallows itself in darkness:

Matthew 10:26
"So have no fear of them, for nothing is covered that will not be revealed, or hidden that will not be known."

Church Alienation

Having been raised in an environment where you never really questioned your church (not out loud at least) and feeling un-Christian if you criticize ministers or church leaders, this is a touchy subject for me. But I discovered my faith equity didn't mean a hill of beans to my church leadership when I was in the middle of Chuck's harassment.

Instead of rehashing what happened to me, I'm going to defer to the experts, and include an excerpt from the book *When Loving Him Is Hurting You* by Dr. David Hawkins, a Christian marriage counselor and well-known author. In Dr. Hawkins' book, he illuminates the ways that emotional abuse takes up residence in marriages and relationships, and how the church tends to protect the abuser instead of the abused:

(Abuse Victims and the Church)

Victims of abuse want to feel the protective sanctuary of a church family and pastor. They need a refuge from the harm of their home. Unfortunately, many don't find a safe, listening ear. Many are met with distant, preachy counsel that leaves them feeling unprotected and even more confused.

Victims of narcissistic and emotional abuse need specialized help. They need friends who will come alongside and offer support and guidance. They need family who will understand and offer love – and lots of it. They need their church family to surround them with compassion and spiritual care.

Tragically, the very institution many women look to for support and encouragement, the church, all too often turns its back on the wounded. Too often the church not only fails to protect abused women but also refuses to hold men accountable for their emotional and narcissistic abuse. Often the church offers men protection while shaming women into going back to the abuse, all in the name of faith.

This creates an unfathomable wound to women.

(excerpt from When Loving Him Is Hurting You, by David Hawkins, Harvest House Publishers, 2007.)

Natalie Hoffman, author of *Is It Me? Making Sense of Your Confusing Marriage: A Christian Woman's Guide to Hidden Emotional and Spiritual Abuse*, offers a research study and blog offering on her website Flying Free Now (www.flyingfreenow.com) that details many of the horrific things said to actual women who were suffering through abusive marriages by either ministers, church leaders, or other church members:

> "All couples fight."
>
> "You are not in God's will."
>
> "You need to give him more sex."
>
> "You're not praying hard enough."
>
> "Do what he wants you to do—whatever makes him happy."
>
> "You made a vow. You have to keep it."

"All marriages are hard."

"If you leave, you don't love your children."

"Are you keeping the house clean enough? Do you cook him good dinners?"

"You had too many babies, so that's why he abuses you."

"Back away from your relationship with Jesus. It intimidates your husband. You must decrease so he can increase."

"IF these things are really going on in your house (and that is a big IF) then it's your responsibility to get him the help he needs."

"You are a slave to Christ and your husband. There is no greater love than to die for your husband. Treat him as if he were God. He stands in the place of God for you."

"Compliment him more. He is discouraged and just needs to be affirmed by someone who thinks he is good looking."

"Quit focusing on the bad stuff. Focus on the WINS!"

"Your personality is too strong. You need to be meek in order to let him shine." (This woman said she tried to be less intelligent, not have opinions, submit, and not use her sense of humor. Basically, become a non-person.)

"He's not complicated, but you are. You need counseling."

"You don't know how good you have it. Be thankful he isn't worse."

"The only right you have is to die to yourself."

"Your husband had an affair with your sister? You need to initiate sex, then. Because love covers a multitude of sins."

"Jesus is pleased with your suffering."

"If your husband is addicted to porn and sleeps with other men and women, it's because you are frigid and unimaginative. Work on that."

"Just because your husband recently cheated on you, and you are nine months pregnant, doesn't give you the right to refuse him sex."

"Remember the reasons you married him."

"Your quest for the truth is damaging your marriage. Stop making him feel bad."

"You're blowing things out of proportion."

"You obviously haven't obeyed him perfectly."

"Because of Eve, you owe him obedience and loyalty no matter what."

"Stop expecting a Hollywood romance."

"When he gets home from having an affair, smile at him."

"Christian marriage is hell. Accept it."

"It's just his sin nature. Give him grace."

"Stop complaining before something worse happens."

"He's not abusive enough for you to divorce him. We can tell."

"Grow a thicker skin."

"Forgive without limit. Respect him."

"You are having problems because you let him have your body before marriage."

"Study Hosea who married a prostitute and stayed no matter what."

"Buy a sexy nightie, and he'll stop sleeping around."

After attempted murder and a sexual assault, her pastor told her "your situation is a 3 out of 10. Let him move back home or you'll be held accountable before God for putting a nail in the coffin of your marriage."

"Repent of your bitterness."

"Churches are exempt from protective orders, so your husband can be here."

"Win him without a word."

"You are obviously mentally ill."

"He's not hitting you. What's the big deal?"

"The word 'abuse' is not in the Bible."

"A man would never treat his wife like this unless she were doing something wrong."

"If you don't stay, you have no faith."

"You aren't a Christian."

"God will kill your child if you leave."

"You don't know what your name is. You are _____'s wife. You have no name."

"It is your biblical duty before God to suffer within your marriage."

My observation personally has been that people will say anything to make <u>themselves</u> feel better, but they change their tune quickly when it's them or a family member being affected. I believe that the reasons behind the lack of support churches have for women in abusive (emotionally, physically, financially, or otherwise) relationships have to do with:

- lack of spiritual courage
- money (the abuser contributes to the church)
- social weakness (popularity, politics, and who's who)
- misogyny on the part of church leadership
- laziness and ignorance

Churches, above all, must grow spiritual courage and lose any hint of sexism. This correction is long overdue. Christ said and did enough to show that He was not a hater of women when He walked on this earth.

Chapter 3: Exposing the Problem

78 Court Appearances and What?

Ariana has been dragged to court over manufactured lies against her now 78 times, always involving her children. The courts won't let the children have a word or speak to their judge. She is not "permitted" to get counseling for her children. Never has there ever been a more dumb, deaf and blind courtroom in the entire northern continent than the one overseeing her cases! Her children are regularly harassed, verbally abused, deprived of sleep and basic care, and their feelings completely disregarded by her ex. This has been going on for years. They are teenagers now, and they still can't have a say in their own lives or get desperately needed counseling.

To a discerning person, especially one with even a shred of common sense, it is clear what her ex, Gilbert, is doing: he is a madman bent on litigating her to death. Apparently, this tactic works just fine for family courts. Built into the law, there is the concept of "expungement" (a chronic case of amnesia). There isn't a mechanism built into the court system to identify patterns. I like to call it the ServPro® effect. ServPro® is a company that cleans up homes and businesses when fires and floods happen. They are the pinnacle of cleanup services for disasters nationwide. Their slogan is: ***Like It Never Even Happened.*** Expungement moves the perpetrator to the ***Like It Never Even Happened*** status in family court. It wipes the slate clean so he/she can start over harassing the victim again.

Attackers can enter court over and over, with a new wild claim each time, and the court tends to treat his or her background in the ServPro® style: ***Like It Never Even Happened.*** The truth can be staring all parties, including the judge, in the face. Whole college educations, savings accounts, and entire mortgages are ruined daily with a lethal combination of judicial blindness and opportunistic money-grabbing. This is the reward system that enables family court to be a tool of abuse.

Yet a judge will frequently rule in the favor of the party who has the resources to continue to propagate this war of attrition. Many of these victims are parents who were stay-at-home moms or part-time workers who sacrificed their careers in order to raise their children in an enriched way; almost always in a mutually consented-to agreement with the other parent. These left-behind parents can easily find themselves in poverty and even separation from their children after divorcing. It is by rewarding this visible arm of domestic abuse that the courts promote bullying, gender bias, and family devastation.

Degrees of Pathology

When O.J. Simpson displayed bizarre behavior after the murder of his wife Nicole and her friend Ron Goldberg in June 1994, I was not aware that I was witnessing narcissistic personality disorder. After researching for many years, I believe that the only thing separating the random raging narcissist from a murderer is simply the degree of pathology involved.

To identify the symptoms of narcissism, one need only look as far as the Diagnostic and Statistical Manual of Mental Disorders:

- A preoccupation with fantasies of unlimited success, power, brilliance, beauty, or ideal love
- A belief that he or she is "special" and unique and can only be understood by or should associate with similar high-status people and organizations
- A need for excessive admiration
- A sense of entitlement or unreasonable expectation of special treatment or extreme loyalty
- A tendency to use others for their own needs or wants
- A lack of empathy, or unwillingness/inability to recognize and honor the needs and feelings of others
- Proneness to envy or having a belief that they are envied by others
- A sense of arrogance shown in behaviors and/or attitudes

- Care quite a bit about their appearance and can come across as quite charming
- Expect to be recognized as superior even without achievements that warrant it, and will discount any evidence that doesn't support their belief of their own superiority
- Exaggerate their own achievements and talents, even to the point of lying
- Are often preoccupied with fantasies about success, power, brilliance, beauty or the perfect mate
- Are highly manipulative
- Tend to project their bad behavior onto others, meaning they may accuse you of the very behavior they are conducting
- Monopolize conversations and belittle or look down on people they perceive as inferior
- Aren't opposed to taking advantage of others to get what they want
- Fail to see or value the needs and feelings of others
- Have no remorse for hurting others and rarely apologize unless it will benefit them in some way
- Insist on having the best of everything and believe that they deserve this
- Aren't able to handle criticism and lash out if they feel slighted in any way

When you combine these patterns with the fallibility of the court system, you have a witches' brew of dysfunction and disaster. Sadly, for some, it is too late before the system realizes what it should have done.

If you listen to the 911 tapes of Nicole Brown Simpson calling police and the ranting and raging O.J. in the background, and I'd imagine most of you reading this book know this person. He doesn't sound any different in the call to me than when Chuck would get wound up. I even see similarities in facial expressions when O.J. continued to spin lie after lie in front of the camera, smiling broadly. In recent years, Simpson proclaimed to a parole board that he had led a conflict-free life. Now he claims to have chronic traumatic encephalopathy (CTE) in order to scapegoat his football career as the cause of his murderous past.

Although it is hard to believe, there are worse pathologies in narcissism than that of O.J. Simpson. I am sure that Nicole, like all mothers, would choose that her life be taken instead of her children, because the life of mourning a child is anybody's worst nightmare. Angels fear to tread where the parents of children slaughtered as "payback" lay their heads each night.

A lifetime of grief overwhelms the parent's life; the batterer has accomplished his or her goal. This unspeakable crime has to be one of the worst evils ever parlayed upon this earth. But the pathology is the same: dominion, control, dictatorship, and winning at all costs.

Kids for Sale

From the limited pool of contributors to this book, we found the following real occurrences of gross ethical misconduct and judicial irresponsibility:

- Family court attorneys offering to "flip" on their own clients in exchange for support in a political race
- A family court attorney representing that a client needed to "pay off" a custody evaluator in exchange for a positive custody evaluation
- A judge-attorney relationship outcome analysis which indicated that an attorney had never lost a case in the judge's courtroom
- Due process obstruction in courthouses by way of not following state laws in assigning cases
- Attorneys who violated attorney client privilege by disclosing private client information to opposing counsel
- Attorneys who violated privacy by disclosing private client information to outside parties unrelated to the case
- A judge who was voted out of office over multiple instances of conflicts of interest, corrupted decision making, and judicial bias against mothers
- A parent who was murdered in part due to a faulty and inadequate line of decision making by a family court judge

- An attorney who refused to acknowledge discovery which proved claims made by his client were wholly false
- A politician attorney who could cause cases not to be heard by using legislative privilege

With an environment like this in family court, is anyone surprised that we suffer lifetimes of financial derailment, grief, and loss of quality of life? The list above is only the tip of the iceberg and doesn't nearly cover all the failings we found.

Until states revamp their enforcement, judge training, and due process, family courts are at risk of being unfairly rigged for the party with either the most money or the most political influence. All children, moms, and dads deserve a fair day in court. Family Court is the most important court in America, because it caretakes our biggest resource – our children.

Feeding the Monster

In the movie Little Shop of Horrors, the adorable little plant grows quickly, and it is charming up to a point. But the more it eats, the more it grows, and the more it takes over the lives of its caretaker, until it must be destroyed, but only after it has eaten most of the characters. **"FEED ME!"** is the famous line associated with the people-eating Venus Flytrap. In the end, it tries to eat everyone.

There are few who would disagree, including many attorneys, that the family court system has become a life-eating monster that is never sated, and its need for cash to feed itself continually grows. It destroys families while it preserves prolific careers for judges, GALs, custody evaluators, attorneys, and court officers.

It doesn't have a brain or a soul, this system. It is merely a name associated with the outer and inner workings of its components. Its market value is whatever the players choose to assign to it, and its sacrifices are the lives of children and good parents. Its rules are ambiguous, its enforcement is weak, and it doesn't have a shred of common sense, either.

It is the only court system in the country that actually promotes double, triple, and quadruple jeopardy. The "accused" can be tried on the same issue over and over. This time, you missed a football practice because of excessive homework, and therefore do not care about your child's extracurricular activities. Next time, it will be the fact that your ex missed a parent-teacher conference, and you were blamed because you did not notify him on *Our Family Wizard* (an app used in co-parenting situations) even though the written calendars and letters went out to each and every parent at the school.

The Monster doesn't care that it is going to cost you $3000 to defend the fact that you are not your ex-husband's enslaved secretary for life, or that you can produce proof from the school office that a copy went out directly to him. ***The Monster*** will formalize the process and suck you into the endless vacuum of filings, expenses, and attorney fees. It is anybody's guess whether the judge will find you guilty anyway.

The mechanism that feeds ***The Monster*** is the symbiance between the abusive filer seeking revenge, and the revenue opportunity (***The Monster's*** voracious appetite) this provides. It is a perfect pairing of maliciousness and greed. Get a screening board in each system to cost-effectively determine which cases have validity? *"Preposterous! That would be far too simple."* Enforce false filings by causing the accusing party to pay the defendant's court costs plus fees? *"No, we can't do that! That would be biting the hand that feeds us!"*

The Monster must be held accountable for its inefficiency and waste, and it must begin to be recognized as an inanimate being without a soul. If it won't accomplish what its mission really should be, then it needs to be disassembled and repurposed, even if that means cutting off its head and starting over. The allure of unlimited fees and never-ending cases is just too strong to evoke an overabundance of ethics on the part of its beneficiaries. How do we start? First, by making its activities and outcomes translucent and accessible. This means that every judge should be subject to data disclosure on how he or she rules, by pattern, potential bias, and by specific cases and representing attorneys. If there is a relationship with an attorney that indicates bias, data will not lie. Does this judge rule overwhelmingly in favor of male plaintiffs? Female plaintiffs?

Data disclosure is only one way to 'call out' ***The Monster.*** Proper screening of cases and enforcement of penalties for phony cases and vexatious litigation is another. Don't worry, ***Monster*** -- there will be plenty of valid cases to provide your treasure trove of cash flow. Now here's a thought – maybe attorneys could ***stop representing liars and abusers!***

Ultimately, state codes must change to make the family court system into what it should be: an enforcer of the best interests of children. In many ways, it could not perform any worse than it does today in accomplishing this. Two main reasons for this is that children are regarded as property to be divided, and parental rights trump the rights of children. As Tina Swithin, founder of the organization One Mom's Battle (www.onemomsbattle.com) has stated acutely of the family court system, "It takes longer to adopt a puppy from the pound than to decide the fate of a child."

The Monster has to go; at the very least it must be defanged. It certainly must need to learn to eat justice instead of children.

Children Defined as Property

If only people only knew how children are weaponized by abusive and narcissistic parents! Those of us who have experienced this firsthand are mortified at the blindness of judges, GALs, and even court officers at the trauma and damage that this devastating action does to the children and the "target" parent, and for how long it is allowed to go on.

When children who have encountered emotional and even physical abuse cannot speak for themselves, it creates another social tragedy beyond the first injury: the loss of hope. To a child, even one day or weekend can bring trauma that seems as if it will go on forever. To a teenager, a month of weekends with an abuser with no relief can lead to thoughts of suicide, self-hatred, and a defeatist mentality that can carry through to adulthood.

When an adult is gaslighted, emotionally or physically abused, there is usually an awareness that the actions against them are wrong. Long stints of having this abuse unpunished and even rewarded by the courts can even cause the most stable adult to no longer believe in their own future, or in justice. Think of how much worse this is in a 13-year-old with no emotional tools.

Combine the hopelessness of never being vindicated with the aloneness of facing an abusive or terminally angry parent, along with the immaturity and innocence of youth, and we can see why inaction by the courts is causing a societal crisis which is so broad in its scope that it cannot be measured. Lost childhoods and the removal of healthy parental relationships inflict permanent damage.

What will it take to get emotional abuse and weaponizing of children classification as abuse in family court? We can attempt to calculate the costs to society and its effect on our culture and economy. It should matter if even one lone parent suffers bankruptcy and the loss of his children as a result of lies and exploitation in the courts.

It would be far easier to integrate these patterns of recognition into judge training delivered by competent professionals who understand domestic abuse by proxy. The cost of doing this effectively would yield a more discerning, mature judge, and a societal savings. This would be translatable to lowered teen suicide, more financial stability and financial opportunity, and increased optimism.

It is not difficult to identify court-mongering plaintiffs. A preliminary, simplified flowchart is presented in the section *Flowchart of Narcissistic Identifiers* in the back of this book as a starting framework to screen for vexatious litigation.

The following poem is directed at emotional batterers who weaponize their children in order to destroy the other parent:

She Isn't a Weapon

She isn't a weapon,
    like a serrated knife;

to thrust into her mother's heart.

She isn't a bullet
    cold and piercing,

to penetrate bone and crush.

She isn't a hammer
    to deliver your justice;

or the quashing of life to your glee.

She isn't a tool of destruction
    to atone for your anger.

Your arrow, your point
    will find her heart instead;

and your dark soul is tragically fed.

by Jess Moravian

Family Court as Phony Theatre

In this analogy, *The Doors* isn't a retro band we all remember. If we've been in a courtroom represented by an attorney in family court, most of us have encountered *The Doors*. Attorneys go in the doors in the courtroom, and they go out of the doors. They elusively disappear and leave their clients shaking in their boots at having to even be in the same room with their abusers and stalkers.

The Doors take different forms. We've seen half-doors in front of a courtroom which swing back and forth with each case being read out loud. We've experienced full doors that go in and out of judge's chambers; where attorneys jockey for position while their bewildered clients wonder what's going on, how much this billing cycle will be, and will they see their kids after court, *ever.*

Big stacks of documents are carried in briefcases and boxes. The papers seem to be weighty props declaring the research and validation of the case the attorney represents. To the clients, they represent thousands of dollars and hundreds of hours of collection time, not to mention cases of printer ink. They also represent the stress of having to live our lives as slaves to the legal libraries we must keep in our spare rooms and closets in which everything we write or receive from the ex is potentially a smoking gun or the key to our own defense.

This life as a slave to the courts turns us into PTSD victims, some of us knowing the difference between homelessness and survival is one phony case filing away.

Are the underlying documents in the stacks actually blank pieces of paper? We'll never know. I was told by one attorney that family court is really just a game, and that struck me in precisely the wrong way. I'd already been fighting Chuck's slander and fake cases for eight years by then.

I didn't see the futures of my children, my worth as a mother, and my financial future as a game. This game benefits a consistent recipient: the attorneys and the attackers. At the end of the day, the billings are high, court is over, and all the court officers, attorneys and judges get to go home without having to face the consequences that their lives that have just been turned upside down.

The other phenomenon that occurs in family court is that no matter what the preparation for the case, a parent can find themselves a victim of negotiation for case presentation order in a badminton game between the judge and the attorneys. It doesn't matter if you, the client, paid an expert witness to show up that day for $500 per hour, or had a vital witness who had taken off from work that day to appear. What will matter that day is which attorney gets his or her way with the judge when they make the claim that their case will "only take a few minutes".

There is no recourse or credit for even a preferentially set trial date, in most cases, and no one seems to care how many thousands of dollars a plaintiff or defendant is additionally charged; not to mention the attorney fees billed to bring the case to the court repeatedly until it is heard. Entire college educations, Christmas mornings, tuitions, and school clothes are sacrificed every day just defending one's right to the freedom to carry on as a parent. Too often, it is the false accusations that win.

The Doors have become such a dreaded component of family court that the following poem is dedicated to the victims of their flawed function:

The Doors

The doors, the doors,
Like judgment hitting the floors;

Swish swash, the hinges swing,
What doom will the bringer bring?

The doors, the doors,
Like children hitting the floors;

The click of the heels
and the fog of the deals,

And the devil will soon be crowned king!

The doors, the doors,
Like treasure hitting the floors;

The papers fly in,
The papers fly out;

And the tally of consequence soars.

The doors, the doors,
Like poor souls hitting the floors;

In the clash of a gavel,
The cheering of lies,

And life as we know is no more.

By Jess Moravian

The Magic Eye

Magic Eye is a series of books in the 90s which allowed people to see 3D images by focusing on patterns. The viewer must diverge their eyes in order to see a hidden three-dimensional image within the pattern. The term "Magic Eye" has become a generic classification often used to refer to those types of images. A MagicEye® image has a repeating pattern that differs slightly with each repetition, therefore giving an illusion of depth when each eye focuses on a different part of the pattern.

I see the patterns of vexatious litigation and harassment likened to the MagicEye® as they relate to the blindness of the courts. The courts *see* perfectly legal filings, representative fees, and "normal" processing of cases. Unfortunately, every day, divorcing families march into court paying thousands of dollars to have their lives served on a silver platter to an attacker by clueless judges and court officers. The courts and officials, and many times the attorneys are not seeing the real picture – the one buried very shallowly beneath the surface.

The pattern beneath the "white noise" of filings is sinister. The wholesale destruction that chronic legal stalking causes can be a "free prison" of lifetime misery. It can appear to an outsider that a victim is living a normal life, but in reality, that parent is captive to whatever the harasser might do next, and sadly, whatever the courts decide to let them do. They can't get ahead in their careers, they are destroyed financially, and they have permanent PTSD from 'combat' in the courts. Understandably, they sometimes lose hope and even have been known to take their own lives.

The legal momentum is almost always in favor of the filer, and most of the time the abuser is the one who has the funds to continue the injury. This type of litigious behavior is applauded in business circles. Savvy litigants are praised for their brilliant strategy and tenaciousness. But when used against parents and children in the most vulnerable of situations, it becomes something else.

This is why I fervently believe that family court code must turn away from the commonality of business law and old tactics of court warfare to refocus itself on the best interests of children. Family court codes have been disconnected from common sense for far too long, and there is no excuse for not recognizing these evil patterns of abuse that reveal the true picture beneath. Family courts need to be able to use the "magic eye" of seeing beyond the surface to the true intent of the filer.

Banana in The Tailpipe

One of my favorite movies lines to use is from *Beverly Hills Cop* when Eddie Murphy fools the cops staking him out and yells, **"I ain't fallin' for no banana in my tailpipe!"** It seems the courts are falling for the 'banana in the tailpipe' of the term parental alienation (PA) still. Ever since abusive parents were clued into this subject matter, they have gravitated to blaming target parents for themselves not having a bond or relationship with their own kids.

One of the classic qualifiers of parental alienation is that the child actually has to be estranged from the target parent. This means that any child who is not allowed visitation with a parent due to physical or sexual abuse could potentially be labeled as 'alienated'. This is partly the reason that the water gets muddied so badly. The system is blind to the issues that caused the child to not want to be with the parent in the first place. The fact is that abusive parents have figured out that parental alienation is a catchphrase that can be used in court to win custody over a healthy parent.

Joan S. Meier's research white paper *Parental Alienation Syndrome and Parental Alienation: A Research Review* points out effectively that PAS can be an opinion offered by a Guardian Ad Litem (GAL) without ever questioning its scientific validity or admissibility. Meier goes on to list some protocols for an abuse-sensitive approach in courtroom settings, among which are:

1. **Assess abuse first.** If abuse claims are validated, then the rest of the evaluation should be monitored with safety concerns first. (We feel this should equally include emotional abuse with the emotional safety of the child factored in.)

2. **Require evaluators to have genuine expertise in both child abuse and domestic violence.** This should go without saying, but sadly, people are brought into cases regularly with no training at all. This point iterated by Meier goes on to point out that assumptions are often made that women's abuse allegations are false.

3. **Once abuse is found, an abuser's claims against the victim should not be considered.** Alienating conduct bound up with a batterer's abuse pattern is part of the abuse and should never be an "assist" to get a child away from a loving parent.

4. **A finding of alienation should not be based on unconfirmed abuse allegations or protective measures by the favored parent.** In other words, claims of alienation should stand alone and separate from claims of abuse. Misusing a claim of alienation to defeat or undermine the seriousness of abuse should never be allowed to happen.

The paper goes on to list other parameters with sound recommendations and to separate what is real in parental alienation claims. Sadly, abusers who get full custody through some court judgment error will actively alienate children from their victim-parent. The claim parental alienation is most commonly used against mothers.

A recent data pull from Westlaw's Litigation Analytics (Thompson and Reuters) yielded a search result of over 1300 current family cases in the U.S. that mentioned parental alienation in the case dialogue. There is increasingly published opinion indicating overuse of parental alienation claims in family court, and the term should be immediately thrown out as an archaic and dangerous tool of batterers.

A recent Huffington Post article about parental alienation as a tool in family court revealed that 72 percent of fathers who accused the mother of parental alienation in court won their cases. The father won 69 percent of the time when child abuse was alleged (against the father) and 81 percent of the time when child sexual abuse (against the father) was alleged. Sadly, because of these and other statistics, many cases of legitimate abuse now go unreported.

Even when an alienating parent fails in court, they don't stop trying to alienate on the home front. My friend Tricia has three adopted children. Her narcissistic ex, Thurman, has worked on one of the children at a time, for years, infusing them with lies that just keep coming. Sometimes Thurman is believed and sometimes he isn't. His sick, pervasive goal is destruction of Tricia's family and life.

His latest conquest is their oldest son who just revealed that Thurman told him that his mother has been stealing his college money. Thurman is so convincing that Tricia's son Ray wasn't checking facts, even though he has been caught at lying numerous times. Sadly, there is nothing to stop Thurman from wreaking havoc on Tricia's life until her children realize that his entire agenda has been a farce.

Chapter 4: Healing in the Maelstrom

Darkness vs. Light

John 1: 4-5
"In him was life, and that life was the light of men.
The light shines in the darkness, but the darkness has not understood it."

During the worst years of my battle, when Ren was suffering the most, and I had to hide counseling to protect him, I felt I was losing my mind and my grip on life. It cannot even be counted how many days I lived paralyzed by fear and worry. Prayer is the only thing that carried me through.

One of the most helpful phrases that I learned through reading and meditating was the phrase, ***"Darkness cannot live in light."*** I repeated this over and over in my head during my worst times. It provided me strength to carry on and to build a safe space around me while I navigated through the myriad of lies propped up by Chuck. There were many instances when I was forced to sit in waiting rooms and physician's offices in close distance with Chuck while he ran his false court campaigns against me. I cannot describe the nausea, panic and PTSD I felt while having to be in his presence.

As you know already, batterers are waiting for you to make one wrong statement or move so that they can bring it before a judge. Chuck smugly knew that I couldn't address the fact that his claims were fabricated. He knew that until the court date, I would have to walk on pins and needles.

The sad part in my case was that Chuck knew in advance that he would win after we lost our very good judge in redistricting, no matter what he did. This situation served as a perfect catalyst for further harassment.

I still think that darkness vs. light and that polarity is an analogy of goodness versus evil, literally. I believe it is the very reason that mentally disordered individuals such as Chuck are attracted to empathetic, honest, and optimistic personality types. I believe that post-separation and post-divorce abuse, particularly using the court systems to harass victims, is a social holocaust.

I wish for you as a survivor of domestic abuse, that your light becomes stronger than the darkness, and I believe this is possible with faith and prayer. Only God knows the answers and special alchemy that will work in your case. Praying nightly for children and for safety of their souls, minds, and hearts is one way to wake up feeling a little more solid even when you are going through the darkest of times.

Wait Am I A Narcissist?

Did you get so tired and confused in your battle that you wondered if you were actually the narcissist? Through all the gaslighting and manipulation, along with the self-loathing that occurs when you are emotionally used up, it is no wonder that we are the ones who sit up at night worrying. I've devised a handy-dandy checklist for you to keep at your bedside for times when you just aren't sure if it isn't you who is the problem:

You Might Be A Narcissist If...

- Your "Mother of The Year" nomination by the school far exceeds the boring and humdrum act of spending quality downtime with your family. Everything you do is a resume item.

- You possess a legion of followers you call friends who will jump to your aid at the moment you call them like a herd of cattle, especially to team up on an adversary.

- You think, "How dare she leave me or think that she is not going to pay for what she has done to ME!" instead of questioning what role you played in her exit.

- You routinely twist the truth and make up situations involving people you seek to harm.

- You really don't think that notice from the IRS or that order from that stupid judge really means you and you are above subjecting yourself to authority.

- Counseling is for those poor souls who just cannot get their act together and are far inferior to you.

- Your children exist not as separate human beings, but as your property, and they are extensions of your goals and aspirations.

- You think: "No one really liked (my ex) anyway which is why (he or she) has no friends. In fact, the only value that my ex-spouse really had was related to the value I brought to the table."

- You can become an entirely different person at the drop of a hat, depending on who you are trying to manipulate for your own gain. You feel that you are so good at this that you will never be caught.

- You misrepresent your ex's name, address, or role in your child's life to prohibit necessary communication from schools, church, or doctors as a measure of control.

- You continually are absorbed in how to destroy your ex or to cause pain and heartache.

- The score must be settled. Every. Single. Time. Legal action has become a way of avenging whatever wrong you feel you've suffered. You don't care how your children will be affected.

You're Probably Not A Narcissist If...

- You actually question whether you are a narcissist and worry about it.

- You've put your kids' needs before your own, countless times, when no one saw you doing it.

- You stayed longer than you felt you could in your marriage to keep your kids emotionally safe.

- You sought counseling on your own to fully understand how to parent better or to deal with your difficult divorce. You think something may be wrong with you. You think you may have caused this awful situation.

- You've been through more than one attorney due of the financial and emotional exhaustion having to go to court repeatedly. Sometimes your attorneys do not understand you or your cases.

- You have a handful of loyal friends who would never bully another person. They are not always the popular ones in social circles.

- You openly care about the plight of others, especially others who have endured emotional abuse.

- You are the same at all times: compassionate, caring, and honest. You do not tell stories that are not true about anyone, including your ex.

- You honor court orders to the best of your ability, and you'd never ignore an IRS notice. You are not above authority.

- You believe in supporting other women or standing up for anyone who is being victimized, even if it means your own social image gets tarnished.

- You don't try to control all the people, teachers, parents and friends your children have. You see your children as completely separate human beings from you. You don't believe that your children are your property.

- You want your children to speak up and you listen to what they have to say. You care about your children's emotional safety and their dreams and aspirations more than your own.

The Five Messages

When compiling this mini storehouse of lessons specifically for those going through the grief and pain of a custody or court battle, God helped me decide on five that were the most helpful. Each of the messages is accompanied by a simple prayer to be modified to your situation:

COMPLACENT WOMEN

I cannot begin to tell you how the words "complacent women" hit me the first time I came across the verse below during my study time:

Isaiah 32:9
You women who are so complacent, rise up and listen to me; you daughters who feel secure, hear what I have to say!

Isaiah 47:8
So now hear this, O lover of luxury, who sits securely, who says to herself, 'I am, and there is none besides me. I will never be a widow or know the loss of children.'

While the words say one thing in the verses, all I can see in my mind's eye are the regular moms (yeah, you know them, the ones not going through a major battle with an abusive ex) fretting over middle school fundraisers, who gets included in PTA email lists, and team selection for pee wee soccer. The main thing on their agenda is going to be deciding where to go for Spring Break (insert eye roll here).

Now, I'm not degrading these women, I'm merely pointing out that for some of us, our thoughts are more like this:

- Do I need medication for the debilitating depression I have?
- Is my narcissistic ex going to gain custody of my children, through some lie or financial harassment by simply dragging me to court over and over?
- Why do I feel so excluded from my <u>own</u> life?
- Can I live through this week?

Those of us who have lived in an environment of negativity and spiritual suffering don't relate well to trivialities. We may come across to others as self-absorbed, serious, or quiet. But what we really are is **<u>hanging on for dear life.</u>**

The message is: Keep walking! You are in a holy place and one day you will dance on the mountain. You are a person of substance, and through this suffering, you have gained empathy, knowledge, and stature with God.

"God, I'm losing patience with these women who don't understand me, or who cast me aside. Please help me grow in grace and find true friends in the midst of my struggle. Thank you for loving me and watching over my family. May I be mindful of Your will in my life."

THE SERMON ON THE MOUNT

There is no message more poignant or directed to those who are downtrodden than the message that Christ gave to the crowds that day. No one there except Jesus -- even the disciples, likely knew the significance of what was being delivered. Certainly, its modern relevance could not have been ascertained:

Matthew 5:2-14
The Beatitudes
² And he opened his mouth and taught them, saying:
³ "Blessed are the **poor in spirit**, for theirs is the kingdom of heaven.
⁴ "Blessed are those who **mourn**, for they shall be **comforted**.
⁵ "Blessed are the **meek**, for they shall **inherit the earth**.
⁶ "Blessed are those who **hunger and thirst** for righteousness, for they shall be **satisfied**.
⁷ "Blessed are the **merciful**, for they shall receive **mercy**.
⁸ "Blessed are the **pure in heart**, for they shall **see God**.
⁹ "Blessed are the **peacemakers**, for they shall be called sons[a] of God.
¹⁰ "Blessed are those who are **persecuted** for righteousness' sake, for theirs is the kingdom of heaven.
¹¹ "Blessed are you when others **revile** you and **persecute** you and utter all kinds of **evil** against you **falsely** on my account. ¹² Rejoice and be glad, for your reward is great in heaven, for so they persecuted the prophets who were before you.

Salt and Light

13 "**You are the salt of the earth**, but if salt has lost its taste, how shall its saltiness be restored? It is no longer good for anything except to be thrown out and trampled under people's feet.

14 "**You are the light of the world**. A city set on a hill cannot be hidden. **15** Nor do people light a lamp and put it under a basket, but on a stand, and it gives light to all in the house. **16** In the same way, let your light shine before others, so that they may see your good works and give glory to your Father who is in heaven.

There is not one single phrase delivered on the planet that I relate to more than the words, *'Blessed are they who mourn, for they shall be comforted'*. In my bitter journey, I sometimes had only this idea to rest my head on at the end of the day. The question is always, "How long, Lord?" and "What is the reason for this?" "Have I gone through this needlessly?"

Unfortunately, I can't answer that question any better for you than I have been able to for me. It is still something I will carry long after this book is published, and my days dissipate into dissolving footprints. It has always made me wonder why some of us end up in cesspools of pain and alienation. Modern-day psychologists sometimes tell us that it's all our own doing.

More specifically, I would like to focus on two other concepts in the beatitudes: the concept of being pure in heart, and what being a peacemaker is. What does 'pure in heart' mean? To me, it means my motivation and intent is free from jealousy, meanness, gossip, or flippancy. My heart is driven by love, respect, and commitment to what is right for myself and for others.

To be a peacemaker is absolutely necessary when ensnared in an evil court battle. No good, kind person would ever cause chaos that they know will affect her children negatively, not to mention the insane waste of funds that could be used for college educations or physical needs. We sometimes find out too late that this is the true source of WHY we left – the narcissist is the antithesis of a peacemaker, and we were actually married to a monster waiting to come into full bloom.

A peacemaker is someone who will stop at nothing to diminish conflict. Unfortunately, people who are peacemakers, just like the bullied child at school, are commonly blamed. In the world of narcissistic abuse, no good deed goes unpunished. Yet this is the message from Christ, to let us know that we are the **Salt and Light**, and that we are walking down a path of grace.

My hope is that we are special creatures, caught up in an epic spiritual tug of war, and that one day we'll be compensated with joy, recognition, and the restoration of our true selves.
Beyond this, we all need to surround ourselves with those who support us, mentor us, and who have humility and grace:

"God please make me a receptacle of your love and your Word and help me to gain an understanding of what it means to be aware, reverent, and pure in heart. Thank You for reminding me that my suffering is not forever."

WINGS OF EAGLES

There is a special kind of tired when you are chronically stalked or harassed. The stalking doesn't have to be just about court; it can be inserted everywhere in your daily life. I remember having to think twice about every single email sent, every doctor's visit booked, even my plans during my own weekends of custody might become fodder for Chuck's haranguing. One wrong word or move, and there might be another court case filed.

There were so many days and weeks that I didn't think I could go on. I thought I would simply faint or die from exhaustion. I wasn't built for constant conflict. I lived for downtime and private time with Ren and Gray, away from the glaring, staring, and perpetual oversight of everything I did. I don't need to say much about the following verse, as I think it speaks for itself, and it remains my absolute favorite after all these years:

Isaiah 40:31
[31] but they who wait for the LORD shall renew their strength;
    they shall mount up with wings like eagles;
they shall run and not be weary;
    they shall walk and not faint.

"Lord, please give me strength to fulfill Your will in my life. I pray for my children and their safety, and that they may know their Purpose for Your glory."

PEARLS BEFORE SWINE

The fact that you gave an abuser any of your time or years is the epitome of the verse below. Getting away is even more time consuming for some of us. You are a daughter of God and you aren't required to continue to give your best to someone who will simply trample on your pearls; the gifts you bring to the world:

Matthew 7:6
"Do not give dogs what is holy, and do not throw your **pearls** before pigs, lest they trample them underfoot and turn to attack you.

When the abuser attacks you after trampling your precious life, you become aware of the message above. You have far better accomplishments to attain, and far nicer people to be associated with. Sometimes, it takes years to free yourself from the dogs and pigs.

One of the lessons that I had to learn was that I was actually the victim, not the perpetrator, when I escaped my marriage. Soon enough, the pig emerged, and started trampling my pearls. But in those years after I realized that my pearls had always been trampled by Chuck in one way or another. Learning to discern who is a pig in your life is one of the great growing-up lessons in a person's life.

"God, spare me from the pigs and the dogs and grant me the wisdom to decide who to spend my time and life with, and who to avoid. I realize that the life you gave to me is a precious pearl not to be wasted on those who are not part of the Plan You have for me."

THE MILLSTONE REPEATED
Broader applications of the "Millstone" reference exist; I can think of instances of children being trained for terrorism with the idea that they will be martyred, children whose lives are lost to trafficking, or those who are abducted or killed.

In this lesson, however, I will focus on the subtleties of the message: derailing a child's self-worth through the self-absorbed intent of an adult. Furthermore, the intent to harm another parent emotionally by using a child is one of the most irresponsible and immature acts there is. The punishment for this, while it doesn't seem to exist in the courts, is staggering from a spiritual standpoint:

Matthew 18:6
But whoever causes one of these little ones who believe in me to sin, it would be better for him to have a great **millstone** fastened around his neck and to be drowned in the depth of the sea.

Depending on the version, the verse may say "sin" or "lead astray" interchangeably. The truth is that God has a plan for each child on this earth, and as adults, we are to take this very seriously. Any child that is under our care is our responsibility to see that nothing obstructs that child's positive view of self, which are the prevailing winds that allow God's will to be accomplished. This goes for YOU, family court judges!

Christ was very specific in His reference to the millstone. So, what's worse than having a millstone around your neck and being cast into the sea? I can imagine the parade of horribles. This verse has special relevance in the arena of parental alienation claims, court harassment, and horridly, when a parent attempts to take all custody away from a caring, solid parent. This is the ultimate injustice to the child.

"God, please help me control my anger at the way that my children have been misled. I pray your watch care over them that they will not be occluded from knowing the Truth. Please protect their brains and hearts from permanent damage."

Your Kids Won't Always See It the Same Way

One of the things I had to learn is that Ren and Gray would come in and out of their awareness and have differing views on what the "weather" was with Chuck. My frustration early on was that Chuck could be believed, and I was questioned, even with a long track record of truth. It was also apparent to me that I got all the flak from Ren and Gray, and Chuck sailed merrily along in oblivion because neither one of them wanted to challenge him.

It took years of reading, counseling, and the study of narcissistic abuse to realize that children who are safe emotionally with one parent but not the other will unleash a lot of their negativity, anger, or raw emotion on the safe parent. This is one reason I feel the years walking across my face, and is a price I've had to pay since being drafted into this spiritual war.

Kids are hard-wired for self-preservation by Mother Nature. If a train was coming, you'd want them to get themselves out of the way before saving you. I think they will also tend to save themselves emotionally first. Sometimes, this means developing coping skills such as burying issues, forgetting certain things ever happened, building convoluted views of the parental relationship, and even an altered sense of reality to help them through. They intrinsically need and want to be loved by both parents. You as a victim of the narcissist will likely be further traumatized by your kids' altered views.

Your Truth is your Truth. No one can take that away from you. "If a tree falls in the forest and no one hears it, did it fall?" Of course, it fell, and this is a meaningful concept to those of us who have had unseen injuries. Our trees are falling every day in silence and we are seen as people who either can't cope, are bitter, or weak, ineffective parents who are not able to just 'get along'. I was told by the aforementioned "shrew-woman" church member that everyone at my church thought I was pathetic. I'll never completely get over that one, as it brings panic to my heart thinking, were they all really talking about me while I served on committees, smiled at people beyond the weeping in my heart, raised funds for the youth group, and sat in church praying to God for help? Then she threatened to ruin me if I ever told anyone what she said.

By that time, I was over the moon in understanding human pain and dysfunction. While I didn't share the instance with anyone except my closest friends as a matter of personal ethics, I didn't need someone to tell me that her words were both crazy and wrong.

Most of us tried very hard very early on in our marriages to make peace with the other parent, and there was nothing we could do to put their fire of anger out. It takes someone who has been through this to fully understand it. And do we really WANT our kids to fully "get it"? I have to say I don't want them to know the full impact of what I carry. I want the cycle of abuse broken in their lives. I want them to marry for happiness and have stellar home lives. If they ever do divorce, I want them to treat their ex-spouses with love and respect, and I want them to know how to do this.

I've learned that I have to live in a separate truth from Ren and Gray because they do have good memories with Chuck, while all of my memories have been wiped from my heart. I now know that Chuck only viewed me as a means to an end. I have to remember that Ren and Gray WERE his goals and he has cultivated his relationship with them in a different way. One of the best things I was ever able to give Ren was the counseling he needed to gain tools to deal with Chuck. One of the main things that a child who is suffering verbal abuse needs is to have an unbiased adult tell them that bullying and screaming is wrong, and that it's not their fault.

One of the tools that the failure of the court system granted Gray and Ren, through the corruption related to one of our cases, is that they will likely never trust attorneys, political figures, or judges. This may serve them well one day. When Gray himself discovered the judge's advertising photo on Chuck's attorney's website, this was enforced even more.

I'm not going to stand here and say that Chuck has zero engaging qualities. He just isn't the same person all the time, depending on the person he is in front of. He changes his colors to fit the situation. He's completely fabricated my life to others, he's fabricated my actions to achieve more custody and control of Ren and Gray. He's lied, cheated, and destroyed trust.

Chuck's ethics are that of anyone's worst enemy; he's physically hurt me and hurt me worse emotionally. All my respect for him (and I still had some at the time I exited my marriage) is gone, and he will remain my stalker, abuser, and a financial deadbeat. He burned it all to the ground.

But I have to realize Chuck may never "burn it to the ground" with Ren and Gray. He is a successful actor, as many narcissists are, and can hold his calm stance for months at a time -- until he doesn't. I had calculated at one time that it was approximately 5-6 months between major outbursts, and usually 16-18 months before he filed a new court case. It was almost like a delayed menstrual period for him. That's why I think "what's wrong with Chuck" is clinical.

Ren and Gray will continue to live their Truth and my most fervent hope for them is that they have seen enough of the differences between anger and fear; honesty and pathological lying; kindness and treachery; and darkness vs. light to carry them through. Ren recently suggested that he was interested in majoring in psychology in college, and I could not mask my joy at hearing this. This was encouragement for me that he would not be steered wrong about dysfunction, and hopefully would be able to avoid narcissism in his adult relationships.

I care more now that I have exited the family court treadmill since Ren is an adult, about the end game -- the one in which years from now, I'm a grandma reading to my grandchildren, and Ren and Gray's childhood difficulties are a distant blip. For me, my painful journey has been a source of richness and depth of soul; a purposeful means of helping others.

The insufferable desire and need for peace are a hallmark of God's grace, actualized in those of us who have the courage to step forward on this dusty road to El Roi. I live on the promise that the *God Who Sees* can give us new eyes that see Him clearly and can capture the vision of a better life.

The Girl in The Photo

I rarely look at my wedding photos. They make me super sad. In them I see a girl who is so young; a girl who is hiding a lot of pain. She's a girl who shouldn't be there at all, and just beginning a productive, happy life. She should be moving, choosing another career, and filing a restraining order.

I see her future, and it's going to be hard, and it won't be for years that she experiences true joy through the birth of her children. I can see the fog of time sweep over her, and I begin to understand the wisdom she desperately needed in her life. I can literally feel the years pass over her, and through to me.

I don't look at Chuck at all in the photo, because his face is a hollow skeleton to me. After years of being demeaned, harassed, lied about, and pursued viciously, there is no one behind that false shell that speaks to me. I don't feel or see anything, and that is my special (earned) mojo.

There are times when I see that girl that I want to yell, "Run! You will suffer needlessly at the hand of that guy standing next to you who doesn't value you!"

All I can do is to reach out across time and see another girl, possibly you. Do you see the girl in the picture? Is it you? Beyond the festivities, pretty invitations, the wedding dress, and guests, what is in that girl's soul? Her dreams? Her preciousness? If you are this girl, it is not too late. Perhaps you are just now deciding you can't go on in your marriage. Maybe you are *years into* a custody battle with a narcissist that is not only bankrupting you financially, but also killing your soul.

Maybe you are even one of the unfortunates (like me) who found that nothing the narcissist did (financial irresponsibility, lying, verbal abuse, stalking, and bullying) would be dealt with due to the magnitude of corruption in the family court system. I can't sweep a magic wand over your situation and make it disappear, or change the past, but I can with certainty say that El Roi, *The God Who Sees*, met me where I was, in a desolate place.

Cry out to Him, girl, and He will see you. I know He will, because He's told me to stand in the gap for you. I hope I can do more than just point in His direction.

Resources

Readings That Soothe and Comfort

In my process of healing, and even in the depths of my grief, I came across many verses and other works that just kept coming back to me. My list grows all the time, so please visit our website at **www.roadtoelroi.com** for more useful writings, encouragements, and scriptures.

When you are exhausted and don't know if you have the strength to carry on:

Isaiah 40:31
But those who wait on the LORD Shall renew their strength; They shall mount up with wings like eagles, They shall run and not be weary, They shall walk and not faint.

When you feel as if what has been done to you will never be recognized:

Luke 8:17
For nothing is hidden that will not be made manifest, nor is anything secret that will not be known and come to light.

When you worry that the deception or abuse of your children will never be exposed and that there will never be retribution:

Matthew 18:6
But whoso shall offend one of these little ones which believe in me, it were better for him that a millstone were hanged about his neck, and that he were drowned in the depth of the sea.

When you need a simple verse to repeat and you are going through slanderous court battles and social alienation:

Psalm 120:2
Save me, Lord, from lying lips and from deceitful tongues.

When you need encouragement that you are on the right path:

Matthew 5:3
The Beatitudes
2 And he opened his mouth and taught them, saying:
3 "Blessed are the poor in spirit, for theirs is the kingdom of heaven.
4 "Blessed are those who mourn, for they shall be comforted.
5 "Blessed are the meek, for they shall inherit the earth.
6 "Blessed are those who hunger and thirst for righteousness, for they shall be satisfied.
7 "Blessed are the merciful, for they shall receive mercy.
8 "Blessed are the pure in heart, for they shall see God.
9 "Blessed are the peacemakers, for they shall be called sons[a] of God.
10 "Blessed are those who are persecuted for righteousness' sake, for theirs is the kingdom of heaven.

11 "Blessed are you when others revile you and persecute you and utter all kinds of evil against you falsely on my account. 12 Rejoice and be glad, for your reward is great in heaven, for so they persecuted the prophets who were before you.

When you need encouragement that your prayers will be answered:

Mark 11:24
Therefore I tell you, whatever you ask in prayer, believe that you have received it, and it will be yours.

The incomparable words of Mother Teresa, when you are hurt and damaged by the things that have been misrepresented about you:

"People are often unreasonable, irrational, and self-centered. **Forgive them anyway.**

If you are kind, people may accuse you of selfish, ulterior motives. **Be kind anyway.**

If you are successful, you will win some unfaithful friends and some genuine enemies. **Succeed anyway.**

If you are honest and sincere people may deceive you. **Be honest and sincere anyway.**

What you spend years creating, others could destroy overnight. **Create anyway.**

If you find serenity and happiness, some may be jealous. **Be happy anyway.**

The good you do today, will often be forgotten. **Do good anyway.**

Give the best you have, and it will never be enough. **Give your best anyway.**

In the final analysis, it is between you and God. **It was never between you and them anyway."**

If you are experiencing parental alienation or are separated from your children by way of court abuse, lies, or deceit:

Mother Teresa's brilliance (again):
"You will teach them to fly, but they will not fly your flight. You will teach them to dream, but they will not dream your dream. You will teach them to live, but they will not live your life. Nevertheless, in every flight, in every life, in every dream, the print of the way you taught them will remain."

Irving C. Tomlinson, "Twelve Years with Mary Baker Eddy, Amplified Edition," pp. 103-104.

"Love is the Father, who is strong in His care for His children and provides for every need. Love feeds, clothes, and shelters every one of His dear ones. Love is a Mother tenderly brooding over all Her children. This Mother guards each one from harm, nourishes, holds close to Herself, and carefully leads along the upward way. Love is a Shepherd who goes forth into the darkness of the night, into the storm and wind, to find the lost sheep. This Shepherd of Love leaves the beaten path, searches the wood and marsh, pushes aside the brambles, and seeks until the lost is found; then He places it within His bosom and returns to heal and restore."

Children of the Gavel is an organization in formation dedicated to making positive change (state-by-state) to the root causes of domestic abuse by proxy and family court abuse. In addition, it is committed to judicial translucency.

While **Children of the Gavel** is in its early stages, it is already adding to its board ethically sound law professionals, advisors, and supporters.

Ultimately, Children of the Gavel intends to provide the following:

- *data transparency and statistics on judicial proceedings*

- *education directed at preventing court disasters that harm children and loving parents*

- *assistance to children and parents harmed by faulty court systems*

- *information on the state of the family court system*

The mission statement of **Children of the Gavel**:

"Children of the Gavel is committed to effecting widescale change to benefit parents and children hurt financially, emotionally, and spiritually by narcissistic and emotional abusers utilizing family court systems."

Children of the Gavel website: **www.childrengavel.com**. A portion of the profits of *Road to El Roi* will be donated to the funding and operation of **Children of the Gavel**.

Flowcharts of Narcissistic Identifiers

The flowcharts on the following pages serve as baseline identifiers for patterns of narcissistic post-divorce or post-separation abuse. Consistencies have emerged that should result in screening processes in the family court being implemented state-by-state.

Mandates need to be generated at the federal level and then filtered down through the states. What constitutes domestic abuse needs to be redefined. The social plague of domestic abuse by proxy has long deserved a full classification within each state family court code.

There are over 711 children who have died as a result of the failure of the Family Court system, (**www.centersforjudicialexcellence.com**) but there are also millions in college funds, savings accounts, and rights to thrive that have been ruined by domestic abuse that is allowed to go on due to the fault of the family court ***monster***. This is a constitutional failure (a party's right to live freely) that is possible through manipulated court actions. One of the measures that would quickly change the "game" is actual accountability for prior violations and lying in family court.

Identifying a filing party as vexatious would be a starting point. Vexatious litigation is defined by legal actions instituted without sufficient grounds and serving only to cause damage to the defendant. Once a parent is classified as vexatious, a screening process with penalties for false filings would greatly reduce the numbers of phony cases.

NARCISSISTIC ABUSE INDICATORS FLOWCHART

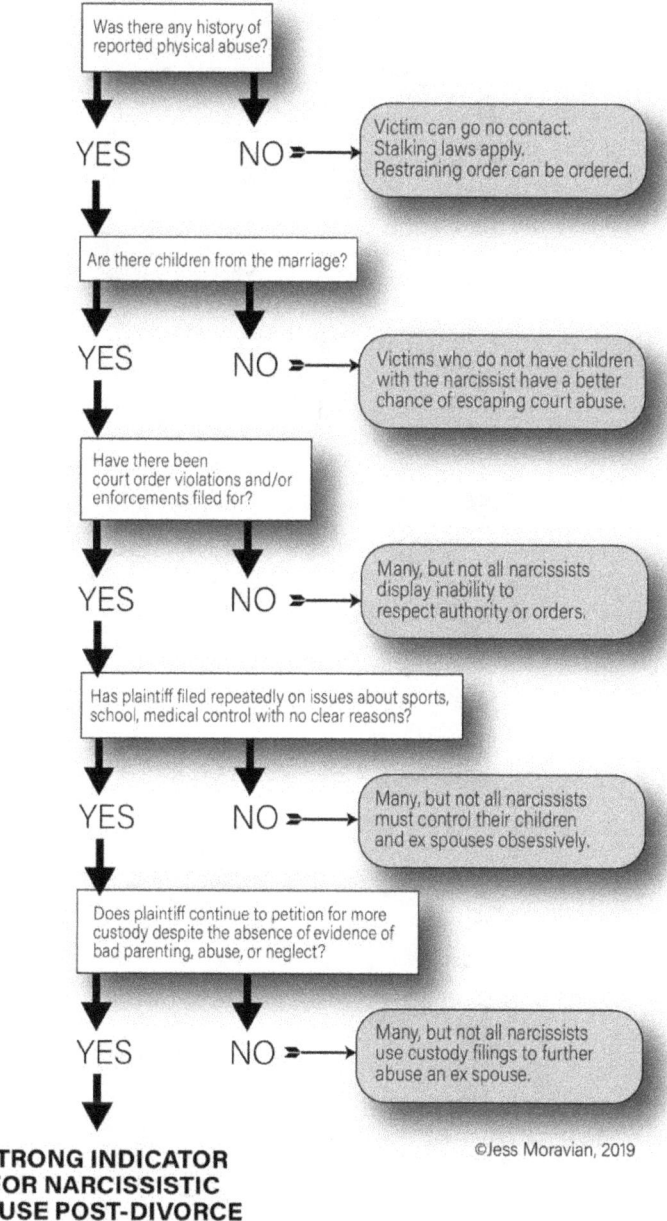

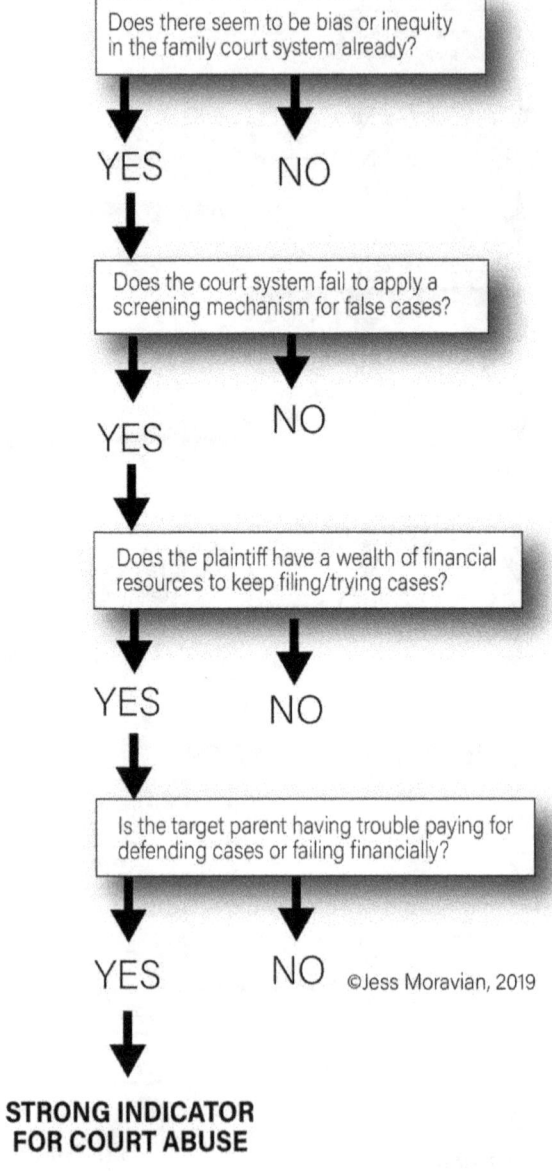

POWER AND CONTROL WHEEL

Physical and sexual assaults, or threats to commit them, are the most apparent forms of domestic violence and are usually the actions that allow others to become aware of the problem. However, regular use of other abusive behaviors by the batterer, when reinforced by one or more acts of physical violence, make up a larger system of abuse. Although physical assaults may occur only once or occasionally, they instill threat of future violent attacks and allow the abuser to take control of the woman's life and circumstances.

The Power & Control diagram is a particularly helpful tool in understanding the overall pattern of abusive and violent behaviors, which are used by a batterer to establish and maintain control over his partner. Very often, one or more violent incidents are accompanied by an array of these other types of abuse. They are less easily identified, yet firmly establish a pattern of intimidation and control in the relationship.

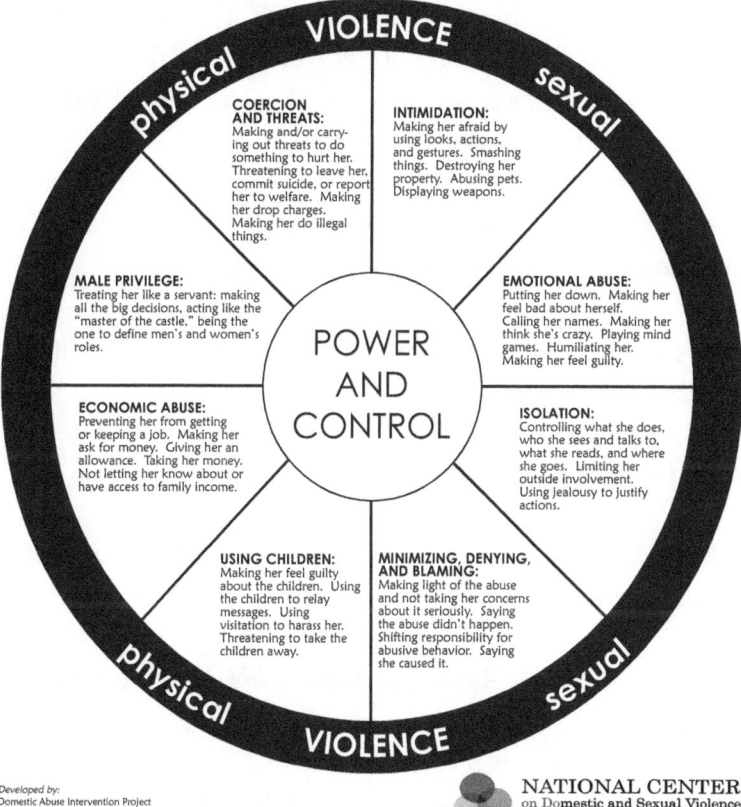

Developed by:
Domestic Abuse Intervention Project
202 East Superior Street
Duluth, MN 55802
218.722.4134

Produced and distributed by:

NATIONAL CENTER
on Domestic and Sexual Violence
training · consulting · advocacy
4612 Shoal Creek Blvd. · Austin, Texas 78756
512.407.9020 (phone and fax) · www.ncdsv.org

Recommended Books

Why Does He Do That? Inside The Minds of Angry and Controlling Men by Lundy Bancroft; Audio, Kindle, Paperback

Boundaries by Dr. Henry Cloud and Dr. John Townsend; Audio, Kindle, Paperback, Hardback

Is It Me? Making Sense of Your Confusing Marriage: A Christian Woman's Guide to Hidden Emotional and Spiritual Abuse by Natalie Hoffman; Audio, Kindle, Paperback

Out of the Fog: Moving from Confusion to Clarity after Narcissistic Abuse by Dana Morningstar; Audio, Kindle, Paperback

Divorcing A Narcissist by Tina Swithin, available in Audio, Kindle, and Paperback

Other Tina Swithin books:

The Narc Decoder: Understanding the Language of the Narcissist; Audio, Kindle, Paperback

Divorcing A Narcissist: Advice from the Battlefield; Audio, Kindle, Paperback

Lemonade Life: A Journal About Managing Life's Lemons; Paperback

Divorcing A Narcissist: Rebuilding After the Storm; Audio, Kindle, Paperback

Movies About Emotional and Physical Abuse

"What's Love Got to Do with It?" (The Tina Turner story) starring Angela Bassett (excellent healing movie).

"Sleeping with The Enemy" starring Julia Roberts (best portrayal of a controlling batterer out there; pay attention to the cans having to face forward in the pantry).

"Gaslight" (1944) starring Ingrid Bergman (where the term gaslighting originated).

"Gone Girl" starring Rosamund Pike and Ben Affleck (female narcissist alert).

"Enough" starring Jennifer Lopez (a must-see if you have ever dealt with both physical and emotional abuse).

"Moonlight" starring Ashton Sanders. (This movie depicts child abuse and domestic abuse/bullying related to a homosexual boy growing up in a stigma-affected black culture.)

"The Girl on The Train" starring Emily Blunt. (Most of us will identify with the behaviors in the movie; however, the pathology of the narcissist is murderous.)

"Diary of a Mad Black Woman" a Madea series film starring Tyler Perry (fun, healthy entertainment if you are a Christian woman on the edge).

Experts and Blogs on Emotional Abuse

Tina Swithin, www.tinaswithin.com and www.onemomsbattle.com

Lundy Bancroft, www.lundybancroft.com

Natalie Hoffman, www.flyingfreenow.com

Dana Morningstar, www.danamorningstar.com

Children of the Gavel, www.childrengavel.com

Road to El Roi, www.roadtoelroi.com

Glossary of Common Terms

Batterer - *a person who uses coercive and abusive tactics and behaviors to establish and maintain power and control over another person with whom the batterer is in an intimate, dating or family relationship. Such behaviors may include, but are not limited to: physical abuse, emotional abuse, financial abuse, spiritual abuse and/or verbal abuse.*

Contempt – *a violation of the terms of a judgement; for example, failing to pay child support or refusing to comply with a restraining order.*

Custody evaluation - *a summary of an investigation into a child's home, family environment, and background, and other circumstances of a child which is used to determine child custody and access during contested divorce proceedings.*

Domestic abuse by proxy - *first defined by Alina Patterson in 2003, domestic abuse by proxy is where a parent with a history of using domestic violence or intimidation uses the child (as a substitute) when s/he does not have access to the former partner.*

Emotional Abuse – *a form of* **abuse**, *characterized by a person subjecting or exposing another person to behavior that may result in* **psychological trauma**, *including* **anxiety, chronic depression**, *or* **post-traumatic stress disorder.**

Flying Monkey - *a flying monkey is someone who does the narcissist's bidding to inflict additional torment to the narcissist's victim. It might consist of spying on the victim, spreading gossip, threatening, or projecting the narcissist as the victim.*

Gaslighting - *a form of psychological manipulation in which a person seeks to sow seeds of doubt in a targeted individual or in members of a targeted group, making them question their own memory, perception, and sanity.*

Grey Rock - *a technique that allows one to take a step back and simply observe instead of fending off or goading into the unwanted attention. Your responses are dull, boring and mundane. Becoming a part of the scenery allows targets to camouflage or fade out. Used successfully against narcissistic personalities.*

Guardian Ad Litem (GAL) - *a guardian appointed by a court to protect the interests of a minor or incompetent in a particular matter.*

Hoovering - *the term used to describe a narcissist trying to re-connect after a time of separation.*

Hypervigilance – *a state of high alert or overreaction to stimuli which can result from post-traumatic stress from narcissistic abuse history.*

Isolation - *when one person uses friends, family and social networks to establish and maintain power and control over a victim. Examples include but are not limited to: controlling where a victim goes, who s/he talks to, what s/he wears, and/or who s/he sees, limiting involvement in places of worship, PTA and other social networks.*

Narcissistic Abuse - *is a form of emotional abuse projected by a **narcissist** on to another individual. Although narcissistic abuse is primarily focused on emotional and psychological abuse, there are other types of narcissistic abuse that can be classified in this category. These include abuses such as financial, spiritual, sexual, and physical.*

Narcissistic Personality Disorder - *a mental condition in which people have an inflated sense of their own importance, a deep need for excessive attention and admiration, troubled relationships, and a lack of empathy for others.*

Narcissistic Supply – *attention the narcissist needs, in both its public forms (fame, notoriety, infamy, celebrity) and its private forms (adoration, adulation, applause, fear, and even repulsion. A person can be a narcissistic supply in the form of the narcissist acting as an emotional vampire (taking pleasure from the victim's pain).*

Parental Alienation (PA)
Parental Alienation Syndrome (PAS) - *Parental alienation syndrome (PAS) is a term introduced by child psychiatrist Richard Gardner in 1985 to describe a distinctive suite of behaviors in children that includes showing extreme but unwarranted fear, disrespect or hostility towards a parent. Recently, PA and PAS have been determined to be misplaced and unfounded ways to remove custody from a healthy parent (see Parental Alienation as a Tool section).*

Post-Traumatic Stress Disorder (PTSD) - *Post-traumatic stress disorder (PTSD) is a mental health condition that's triggered by a terrifying event — either experiencing it or witnessing it. Symptoms may include flashbacks, nightmares and severe anxiety, as well as uncontrollable thoughts about the event. While formerly associated with combat trauma, PTSD is emerging as a consequence of narcissistic and court abuse, as well as stalking and harassment.*

Power and Control Wheel - *The original Power and Control Wheel and Equality Wheel were developed by Domestic Abuse Intervention Programs in Duluth, MN. The Power and Control Wheel is a tool that helps explain the different ways an abusive partner can use power and control to manipulate a relationship.*

Pref set (Preferentially Set) – *when a case that has been granted a priority status for being heard on a certain date due to vital witness testimonies or specific date arrangements of other evidence. Pref set cases, however, find themselves the victims of chaotic court situations in which the preferentially set case is often usurped by the verbal negotiations between judges and attorneys at trial.*

Pro se - *Litigants or parties representing themselves in court without the assistance of an attorney are known as pro se litigants. "Pro se" is Latin for "in one's own behalf."*

Therapeutic Counseling – *When counseling is ordered or agreed to as limited to "for the good of the clients" but the findings cannot be used in custody evaluations or for legal action. A common way for emotional abuser's attorneys to keep findings from being conveyed to the court. Applicable in some state codes.*

Verbal Abuse - *is the act of forcefully criticizing, insulting, or denouncing another person. Characterized by underlying anger and hostility, it is a destructive form of communication intended to harm the **self-concept** of the other person and produce negative emotions. Verbal abuse is a maladaptive mechanism that anyone can display occasionally, such as during times of high stress or physical discomfort. For some people, it is a pattern of behaviors used intentionally to control or manipulate others or to get revenge.*

References

Althouse, Ann. (1992). *Beyond King Solomon's Harlots: Women in Evidence.* 65 S. Cal. L. Rev. 1265. Retrieved from: https://media.law.wisc.edu/m/zkzy2/althouse_beyond_king_solomons_harlots_65_s_cal.pdf

Ashe, Marie. (1991). *Abortion of Narrative: A Reading of the Judgment of Solomon.* Yale Journal of Law & Feminism. Volume 4, Article 11. Retrieved from: https://digitalcommons.law.yale.edu/yjlf/vol4/iss1/11/

Center for Judicial Excellence. (2019). U.S. Divorce Child Murder Data, 2008-present. Retrieved from https://centerforjudicialexcellence.org

Cloud, Dr. Henry, and Townsend, John. 1992, 2017. *Boundaries: When to Say Yes, How to Say No, To Take Control of Your Life.* Zondervan/Harper Collins Publishing.

Endicott, Marisa. (June 14, 2017). *How Parental Alienation Syndrome is Changing Custody Cases Across the U.S.* Retrieved from Huffington Post: https://www.huffpost.com/entry/how-parental-alienation-syndrome-is-changing-custody_b_5939d367e4b094fa859f1719?guccounter=1

Hawkins, David. (2017). *When Loving Him is Hurting You.* Harvest House Publishers.

Hoffman, Natalie. *Is It Me? Making Sense of Your Confusing Marriage: A Christian Woman's Guide to Hidden Emotional and Spiritual Abuse.* (2018). Flying Free Media.

Hoffman, Natalie. (August 11, 2019). Flying Free Now website (www.flyingfreenow.com). *Why the Church Rejects Emotional Abuse and What You Can and Can't Do About It.* Retrieved from **https://flyingfreenow.com/why-the-church-rejects-emotional-abuse-victims-and-what-you-can-and-cant-do-about-it/**

Kligler, Rabbi Jonathan. (August 17, 2017). *Hagar The Stranger from Reconstructing Judaism:*
http://www.reconstructingjudaism.org/sermon/hagar-stranger

Kramer, Wendy, and Cahn, Naomi. (2013). *Finding Our Families: A First-of-Its-Kind Book for Donor-Conceived People and Their Families.* Penguin Group Publishing.

Luciano, Lilia. (May 10, 2018). The Problem with Family Court. ABC10 News:
https://www.abc10.com/article/news/local/abc10-originals/the-problem-with-family-court/103-550687204

Meier, Joan. (September 2013). Parental Alienation Syndrome and Parental Alienation: A Research Review. National Online Resource Center on Violence Against Women:
https://vawnet.org/material/parental-alienation-syndrome-and-parental-alienation-research-review

Morningstar, Dana. (2017). *Out of the Fog: Moving from Confusion to Clarity After Narcissistic Abuse*. Morningstar Media. **(www.danamorningstar.com)**

Narcissism and Narcissistic Personality Disorder. Retrieved October 2019 from Wikipedia Encyclopedia: **https://vawnet.org/material/parental-alienation-syndrome-and-parental-alienation-research-review**

Swithin, Tina. (2012). *Divorcing A Narcissist: One Mom's Battle*. Tina Swithin, LLC. **www.onemomsbattle.com**

Swithin, Tina (2014). *Divorcing A Narcissist: Advice from the Battlefield*. Tina Swithin, LLC. **www.onemomsbattle.com**

Swithin, Tina (October 14, 2013). Narcissistic Personality: Disorder in the Family Court System. Retrieved from: **https://www.onemomsbattle.com/narcissistic-personality-disorder-in-the-family-court-system/**

Genesis 21:8-21 New International Version (NIV)

Hagar and Ishmael Sent Away

⁸ The child grew and was weaned, and on the day Isaac was weaned Abraham held a great feast. ⁹ But Sarah saw that the son whom Hagar the Egyptian had borne to Abraham was mocking, ¹⁰ and she said to Abraham, "Get rid of that slave woman and her son, for that woman's son will never share in the inheritance with my son Isaac."

¹¹ The matter distressed Abraham greatly because it concerned his son. ¹² But God said to him, "Do not be so distressed about the boy and your slave woman. Listen to whatever Sarah tells you, because it

is through Isaac that your offspring[a] will be reckoned. ⁱ³ I will make the son of the slave into a nation also, because he is your offspring."

¹⁴ Early the next morning Abraham took some food and a skin of water and gave them to Hagar. He set them on her shoulders and then sent her off with the boy. She went on her way and wandered in the Desert of Beersheba.

¹⁵ When the water in the skin was gone, she put the boy under one of the bushes. ¹⁶ Then she went off and sat down about a bowshot away, for she thought, "I cannot watch the boy die." And as she sat there, she[b] began to sob.

¹⁷ God heard the boy crying, and the angel of God called to Hagar from heaven and said to her, "What is the matter, Hagar? Do not be afraid; God has heard the boy crying as he lies there. ¹⁸ Lift the boy up and take him by the hand, for I will make him into a great nation."

¹⁹ Then God opened her eyes and she saw a well of water. So she went and filled the skin with water and gave the boy a drink.

²⁰ God was with the boy as he grew up. He lived in the desert and became an archer. ²¹ While he was living in the Desert of Paran, his mother got a wife for him from Egypt.

"If we are created in the Divine image, then we must find in ourselves the capacity for mercy, the capacity to hear the cry of the powerless and to respond with care."

Rabbi Jonathan Kligler
from Hagar the Stranger

A portion of the purchase of this book helps fund
Children of the Gavel (www.childrengavel.com).

www.ingramcontent.com/pod-product-compliance
Lightning Source LLC
LaVergne TN
LVHW091250080426
835510LV00007B/192